Letters from Linton

Letters from Linton

Charles Hofman

Copyright © 2004 by Charles Hofman

All rights reserved. No part of this book may be reproduced or transmitted in any form or by any means, electronic or mechanical, including photo copying, recording, or by any information storage and retrieval system, without permission in writing from the author.

Library of Congress Control Number: 2004092451

ISBN: 0-9753994-0-3

Cover photo: The Orange Grove House of Refuge (Courtesy of Delray Beach Historical Society)

Second Printing

Published by the Delray Beach Historical Society

In memory of

Adolf and Anna Hofman

*"They work from strength to strength
until they stand before God in Zion."*

Psalm 84:7

Acknowledgments

I wish to acknowledge the people who so willingly gave their time and support to this project. Special recognition and thanks go to Dorothy Patterson, Delray Beach Historical Society Archivist, for her steady encouragement, advice, and many hours of consultation. Her expertise facilitated my research immeasurably. I also wish to thank the Delray Beach Historical Society for its encouragement and enthusiastic support.

Another debt of thanks goes to Dorothy Zill Susleck, a Delray Beach native, for her support and gracious cooperation in sharing the autobiography of her grandmother, Sophie Frey, and the diary of her daughter, Carrie Frey.

To Marcia Miller, Trinity Evangelical Lutheran Church Archivist, for her interest and help during the project. To John Reis for his involvement and his research in Dade County deed books and property records.

To translators Fritz Hofmann and Nicholas Babzien, who did the bulk of translating Adolf's letters. Thanks also to Alma Rehard for additional translation work.

To Beverley Longmire, Joyce Summerson, and Jennifer Strickman for editing the entire manuscript and offering suggestions.

A special debt of thanks goes to my cousin Richard Summerson, who helped me recall and recreate memories of our grandparents Adolf and Anna. Above all, my deepest gratitude and thanks go to my wonderful wife Sue for listening to and reliving the history of Linton and Delray Beach over and over again.

Contents

Adolf's Background and Early Life 2
Dreams of Adventure 5
The Lure of Florida 6
The Quest for Land in South Florida 9
Arrival in the Linton Area 10
The Settlement of Linton 14
Anna's Background and Early Life 22
Surviving in Early Linton 24
Early Mail Service 28
Adolf's Acquisition of Land 33
The Hofman Homestead 46
Hofman's Early Real Estate Ventures 66
Sophie Frey - Pioneer Settler 95
Life at Home 104
The Haden Mango 109
The 1903 Hurricane - The Inchulva Disaster 111
Acquiring Additional Farmland 118
Religious Life 123
Delray's Racial and Ethnic Diversity 141
The Yamato Colony 143
Delray Farmers and the Florida East Coast Railway 144
Community Involvement and the Bank of Delray 156
Paul A. Dreher - Dreher Park 173
Land Development - The Florida Boom 179
The Arcade Building 194
Hofman's Development of Delray Neighborhoods 202
The 1928 Hurricane 206
Later Years 215
Requiem 217
Epilogue 220

Preface

...The year was 1895. A German immigrant named Adolf Hofman had just arrived in South Florida. His eyes surveyed the lonely scene before him. A dark labyrinth of mangroves lay tangled along the canal. The deserted shoreline stretched for miles beneath the scorching Florida sun. Broken seashells and fragments of coral bleached by the sun lay abandoned on the shore. The overwhelming silence that surrounded the outpost of Zion was broken only by the strident cry of sea gulls. Even though he was a stranger in a far-off land, he knew he would make this place his home...

Southeast Florida in 1895 was a primitive frontier infested with rattlesnakes and covered with scrub brush and palmettos. Braving the frontier, a few intrepid settlers had established isolated homesteads scattered along the coast. Several speculators had purchased enormous tracts of land and were luring new settlers by advertising land sales.

Determined to acquire land of his own, Adolf Hofman had joined a small group of men in 1895 and ventured to a lonely outpost on Florida's southeast coast. Here Hofman helped establish the town of Linton, known today as the city of Delray Beach. As one of the first pioneers to clear the land, he helped carve Linton out of a morass of swampland and saw palmettos. One of the few original settlers to remain a permanent resident, Hofman acquired more and more land and helped transform Delray Beach from an untamed wilderness into a thriving community.

At first, the town of Linton stood virtually alone, struggling to overcome a hostile environment and economic setbacks. It stood apart from other emerging towns as a result of a close-knit unity forged by the tenacious settlers who managed to survive. Linton was primarily an agrarian town, and for decades Delray Beach continued to be known mainly for its agricultural productivity. Various races and ethnic groups worked together in the fields, creating a sense of pride and community. Although it drew a chic winter colony of artists, writers, and socialites in the 1930s, Delray Beach remained a small town of unassuming residents who knew and cared for each other.

Delray Beach still stands apart from the other cities clustered along Florida's southeast coast. While other cities have succumbed to the sprawl of suburban malls, Delray Beach has retained its distinctive charm by preserving its small town atmosphere. Graced by the Gulf Stream, which sweeps close to its shore, Delray Beach is a casual, subtropical town. Its meandering lanes and quiet neighborhoods display a diverse architectural heritage and add to the picturesque ambiance of a village by the sea. The local respect for historical preservation is seen in the restoration of Old School Square, the designation of historic districts, and the commitment of the Delray Beach Historical Society. As a result of its unique heritage, Delray Beach harbors a rich history of pioneer life and lore.

Letters from Linton is the story of the Hofman legacy told primarily in the form of letters written by Adolf and Anna Hofman from 1895 through 1928. Their story is illustrated with photographs from the Hofman album and the Delray Beach Historical Society. My research in the Delray Beach Historical Society's Cornell Archives room led to other firsthand sources. Archivist Dorothy Patterson directed me to an unpublished collection of interviews conducted with early settlers. Dorothy Zill Susleck, a Delray Beach native, graciously shared the unpublished autobiography of her grandmother, Sophie

Frey, a pioneer settler, and the diary of her mother, Carrie Frey. *Letters from Linton* is not intended to be a comprehensive history of early Delray; instead, it is a personal account of Linton's history seen through the eyes of those who lived it and wrote about it in their letters and journals. The names, dates, and events they mention are historically accurate.

The idea of using letters to narrate the Hofman history grew largely out of childhood memories of visiting my grandparents, Adolf and Anna. Their plain yet imposing home was secluded beneath towering coconut palms and sheltered by a canopy of mango trees. Adolf and Anna had come to the area as German immigrants in 1895, and the stark interior of their house, built in 1896, continued to reflect a pioneer austerity. The smell of varnished wood and the methodical ticking of old clocks evoked an aura of the past that enveloped me on every visit. Regardless of the season, the house always seemed fragrant with the lingering smell of ripe mangoes.

Sooner or later during each visit, our family custom was to gather in the small parlor of the old house to listen to the reading of letters written by our relatives in Germany. Although never commanded, we children tacitly understood that listening to these letters was expected of us.

So we sat quietly for endless periods of time without moving from the old sofa that was tucked under the stairs. I counted the minutes as they slowly ticked by on the antique wall clock, patiently awaiting its chime at each half-hour interval. Since my grandfather was completely blind in his later years, his eldest daughter, my Aunt Annie, would shuffle the pile of letters on her lap and begin the laborious process of reading each letter aloud in German. Struggling to decipher handwriting in a foreign script, Aunt Annie intoned each phrase in her faltering German. Next, she translated each letter from German to English for us, sentence by sentence. Her pronunciation of German was sternly corrected, when needed, by my grandfather, who remained resolute and authoritarian to the end.

The resonance of German commanded awe and added weight and dignity to the letters. I was enthralled by the deep-throated sounds and rhythmic cadence of the foreign tongue, which added mystery to the words. Hearing those doleful letters from the war-torn forties left a lasting impression and reminded me of the continuing link my grandparents had with their fatherland.

More than half a century later, a second cousin, Fritz W. Hofmann of Buckenhof, Germany, was sorting through family documents and papers in the ancestral Hofmann home. By chance, Fritz discovered a thick packet of old letters. To his surprise, some of the letters were over one hundred years old. He was more amazed to discover that these letters described adventures in America in a small town named Linton. These mementos were letters Adolf had written home to his father and to his brother, Gottlieb Friedrich Hofmann, who was Fritz's grandfather. These letters from Linton had been carefully saved. Fritz translated the letters from German to English and sent the original manuscripts along with the translations several years ago.

Both Adolf and Anna wrote frequent letters to relatives in their fatherland describing their lives in Linton as it evolved into Delray Beach. The letters selected to form the heart of this book are presented in chronological order from 1895 through 1928. Although Anna's letters no longer exist in manuscript form, they have been recreated from the notes and entries she wrote in her *Christliches Vergissmeinnich* (Christian Forget-me-nots), a daily diary and calendar book with Bible verses and prayers. These yearly diaries of hers are still in the Hofman family. Anna's grandsons, Richard Summerson and I, recalled stories she told about the past and wove them into the letters. Our memories of her enduring spirit are also included in these letters.

Adolf's letters reveal his desire to settle in the remote frontier of South Florida, his quest for land, and his resolution to remain in Delray despite discouragement and financial setbacks. Anna's letters reveal her gentle spiritual nature triumphing over the harsh realities of frontier life. *Letters from Linton* is the story of one family's struggle to wrest a livelihood from the land that was Linton.

Das Deutsche Emigranten Haus,
No. 26 State St., New York.

Gegründet von der Luth. Emigrantenhaus-Association
von New York 1873.

Pastor W. Berkemeier, Missionar.   John Ostermann, Hauswirth.

Diese Anstalt dient als christliche Herberge zum Schutz und Wohl der Ein- und Auswanderer.

Verkauft Schiffskarten von und nach Europa auf den besten Dampferlinien zu den billigsten Preisen.

Besorgt Geldsendungen unter sicherer Garantie portofrei nach allen Theilen Europa's.

Die Adressen der mit dem Hause in Verbindung stehenden und sehr zu empfehlenden Vertrauensmänner in den Hauptheimstätten sind folgende:

In Bremen: Herr Past. Cuny, an St. Pauli; Herr Missionar H. Kroos, Langen Straße, No. 32.

In Hamburg: Herr Pastor P. Müller, Alte Gröninger Straße, No. 13.

In Stettin: Herr Missionar Blank, Jude Straße, No. 8.

In Antwerpen: Herr Missionar H. Eisenberg, Place du Rhin 7.

In Rotterdam: Herr Missionar Traubel, Boompjes, No. 55.

New York, den 23. Aug. 1895

Meine Lieben!

> *Adolf's first letter home was written from the German Emigrants House in New York City on August 23, 1895. The sentence structure in Adolf's letters is the result of a literal translation of German to English.*

The German Emigrants House
No. 26 State St., New York

New York, Aug. 23, 1895

My Dear Ones,

Until now I fared quite well. I liked it very much on the boat. A few times we had strong winds when we were tossed about quite heavily and finally also got seasick. There were six of us who didn't get seasick right away, and we laughed at the others, but on the sixth day it caught us, too, and how! We didn't care if we lived or died, but fortunately, we had only one day of being seasick.

The beautiful view we had from the ship as we arrived in New York was truly wonderful. We arrived on Wednesday evening in New York but didn't leave the boat until Thursday. We were all examined and questioned so thoroughly that it took us till afternoon to get to our lodging.

We are very well satisfied with this house. Both the food and the beds are excellent. So today I shall travel on. A farmer who returned from a visit in Germany tried to engage me, still on the boat, to go with him. He had a very large farm, and all I would have had to do was to supervise his helpers. But another man advised me against it and told me I would not be safe there because he thought that farmer had such a mean gang of workers that a German beginner would hardly be able to work with them.

I will not write soon again but rather when I know something more definite.

Yours,
Adolf

Adolf's Background and Early Life

Adolf Hofman, christened Wilhelm Adolf Hofmann, was born on April 13, 1871, to Johann Jakob Hofmann and Christine Schwarz of Mönchhof, Germany. He was from a family of eleven children, three of whom died shortly after birth. Of the eight living children, four were boys. Adolf was brought up to work on the family estate.

The Hofman family, originally residents and farmers in Reippersberg, Germany, can be traced back to 1787. Adolf's grandfather moved from Reippersberg to the small farming community of Mönchhof about thirty-five miles north, northeast of Stuttgart in the mid 1800s. His grandfather lived in a large, comfortable, three-story

Adolf's birthplace, the village of Mönchhof, Germany, is located about thirty miles northeast of Stuttgart. (Unless otherwise noted, photographs are from the Hofman family album.)

farmhouse in Mönchhof, which also became the village guesthouse, affording food, drink, and overnight accommodations. Adolf's father, Johann Jakob, likewise continued as a farmer and innkeeper in Mönchhof and occupied the family home with his wife and eight children. The family also owned extensive forests and enjoyed a comfortable living with the added income from this source. With their large farm and lucrative forest acreage, the Hofmanns considered themselves a prosperous and comfortable family. The same ancestral home and farm are still in the Hofmann family today, owned and operated as a gasthaus by Kurt Hofmann, the great-grandson of Johann Jakob.

At fourteen, Adolf was confirmed in his family's religion, the Evangelical Lutheran faith, on April 19, 1885. His Christian faith and his participation in the Lutheran church remained an essential part of his life even after his immigration to America, where his leadership was instrumental in founding Trinity Evangelical Lutheran Church in Delray Beach.

As a boy, Adolf was accustomed to working with his father on the family farm and forest lands. Hard labor, firm family discipline, and the Christian religion formed his values and shaped his outlook on life. Yet Adolf was a restless man, an adventurer, always eager to travel about and seek new challenges.

At the age of eighteen, Adolf attended the *Landwirtschaftlichen Winterschule* (Agricultural Winter School) in Schwäbisch Hall, northeast of Stuttgart. There he excelled in mathematics, surveying, agriculture, and animal medical science. The administrator of the agricultural school, Herr Rindt, rated Adolf's diligence and behavior as very good. In addition, Adolf was awarded a prize for excellence by the Royal Central Office for Agriculture in Württemberg.

Having graduated April 3, 1890, Adolf was employed for a year and a half as an overseer and supervisor on an estate in Kirchheim am Ries in the county of Neresheim. In October of 1891, Adolf left this estate of Herr Adlung to fulfill his military duty.

Once he completed his military obligation, Adolf obtained a position as supervisor of the estate of Baron Heinrich Einem from November 1893 to June 1894. A letter of reference praises him for his "good knowledge of cattle and pig breeding and the care and rearing of horses." From June 25, 1894 to July 19, 1895, Adolf served as an estate supervisor in Alteburg, near Reutlingen. In a letter of reference, the local councilor of agriculture wrote, "Hofmann has earned my fullest satisfaction during that time as a diligent, faithful, and always even-tempered man. He is also even-tempered in his treatment and guidance of those entrusted to his care." During this time, Adolf courted and married a woman by the name of Anna Maria Dreher, who lived in a small village near Reutlingen.

Dreams of Adventure

Adolf had a strong streak of independence and a desire to take charge of his life. His restlessness and longing for adventure were voiced many times to his father. At times, Adolf wanted to travel to Palestine and settle there as a farmer, urged on by letters from a friend who had located there. At other times, he was eager to journey to Africa to join with fellow countrymen and become a surveyor in the German colonies there. After listening to Adolf's plans many times, his father advised him to try his luck at farming in America, where at least he would have a relative to introduce him to the ways of that land. Adolf's mother had a brother, John G. Schwarz, who lived in Jerseyville, Illinois. He had twenty-five acres of farmland and was also the vice-president of the Jerseyville Electric Light, Gas and Power Company.

While in agricultural school in Germany, Adolf heard about fertile land in Florida and dreamed of the possibility of immigrating there. In the summer of 1895, he visited his brother Gottlieb Friedrich in Stuttgart, and, encouraged by being granted a portion of his inheritance early from his father, made arrangements to embark to New York City in August of 1895. Armed with years of farming expertise, encouragement, and capital, Adolf departed from the port of Bremen aboard the ship *Havel* on or about August 8, 1895, in his quest for independence. With him were four reference affidavits, or letters of recommendation, from the estate owners for whom he had worked as supervisor over the years. These letters of reference would serve him well in the new world. On board the steamship, he once again heard fabulous stories of the marvels of South Florida touted by real estate salesmen who plied emigrants with tales of fertile land available at inexpensive prices.

The Lure of Florida

As Adolf mentioned in his letter written from the German Emigrants House, he arrived in New York City on August 22, 1895. Once in America, he took his father's advice and traveled to Jerseyville, Illinois, to stay with his uncle John Schwarz in order to learn the English language and acclimate himself to American ways. Adolf was favorably impressed with the abundance of crops and the large, rolling farms of the Midwest.

His uncle, engrossed in his growing responsibilities as vice-president of an electric and gas power company, had sold off much of his farm and retained only twenty-five acres worked by tenant farmers. During the brief period Adolf stayed with his uncle, he realized that the Schwarz farm was too small to support yet another tenant, much less supervisor, so he began to look for other opportunities in agriculture and the chance to purchase his own land.

Once more, Adolf saw that true opportunity lay in the frontier areas of America where untilled land and unknown adventures awaited. His heart was set on realizing his ambitions.

Weekly advertisements promoting land and seeking settlers in far-flung places such as Florida flooded the area. Fliers promised vast tracts of land in Florida for reasonable prices and dramatized the kind of opportunity and adventure that he was seeking.

Adolf corresponded with a fellow German in Florida and decided to stay with him while searching for suitable land there.

Adolf's second letter home was written from his uncle's farm in Illinois.

Jerseyville, Illinois, Sept. 22, 1895

My Dear Ones,

After I landed in New York, I met a man who was a general agent for a large company that bought land from the State of Florida and is presently improving it by a canal, which costs them forty million dollars. This agent, of course, wanted to persuade me to buy land there immediately, but, needless to say, I declined since I will not buy any land I have not seen before. When I told him that I might go to Florida on an employment basis, he couldn't give me an answer but took me to a partner of his company where I had to show my letters of recommendation. His partner told me that some other partners of the company were keeping land for themselves in order to plant it. But they would not plant it themselves and were looking for a man who would cultivate it for them. My letters of reference were to his liking, and he told me he would present the matter to the president of the company, who would respond in writing. After a long wait, I got the answer that they offered me the job.

In the meantime I obtained more information from Speidel's cousin, who wrote me two letters, saying he doesn't think the company's land is very good. If I wanted to settle in Florida, I had better not buy the company's land but rather join him and stay with him till I find land suitable to buy. I decided to accept his cousin's offer.

So on October 1, I'll leave for Florida.

I like it very well in America so far, especially here, staying with Uncle. It is very interesting for a German to get to know American life and doings. One has to admit that Germany is far behind. There is such a huge crop of corn and fruit in America this year that it is hard to believe. But what good does it do when prices are next to nothing. They leave the fruit to rot on the trees or herd their pigs into their gardens. Uncle, too, has a large abundance of fruit and leaves it to rot. I picked the best of it and stored it in the basement. Uncle still owns his old farm, which is about twenty-five acres. On the farm he has quite good tenants who have one horse, one cow, some pigs, and over one hundred chickens. Uncle kept his old horse, which he uses to drive into town every day to his electrical factory, in which he takes a colossal interest.

My best times in America are probably over by now and things will get more difficult for me after I leave Uncle. If only I knew just a little English it wouldn't be so bad. Germans who know English are ashamed to speak German. Since I can't write you my future address yet, you'll have to address any letters to me to Uncle, who will forward them to me.

        Many greetings,
        Yours,
        Adolf

The Quest for Land in South Florida

One of the people promoting land for sale in South Florida was Captain George Gleason. He had purchased large tracts from the United States Government in 1868 for $1.25 an acre under the Homestead Exemption Act. Captain Gleason advertised his land for $25 an acre. Reading these promotional notices rekindled Adolf's desire for owning land. He had always been an adventurer and a risk taker.

As Adolf mulled over the possibilities promised by Gleason's offerings, he read other land sale notices placed in newspapers by William S. Linton of Saginaw, Michigan. Linton, a persuasive promoter and salesman, had already scouted land in South Florida with his close friend David Swinton in 1894. Linton seized the chance to buy a portion of Gleason's land for development and future resale. With the financial backing of Swinton, Linton made a down payment on 640 acres of Gleason's land at $25 an acre.

Adolf saw Linton's promotional notices and read once again the glowing descriptions of primitive South Florida waiting to be discovered and developed. Linton's newspaper ads fired Adolf's curiosity even further. The advertisements placed by Gleason and Linton confirmed the tales about South Florida that Adolf had heard in agricultural school and on board the steamship. He was the first to respond to Linton's notices with further inquiries (Farrar, 13). The quest for his own land and permanent settlement became more pressing since Anna had just given birth to their first child in Germany on September 17, 1895. His mind was made up, and on October 1, 1895, he left the comfortable farmland of Illinois for the untamed wilderness of South Florida.

Arrival in the Linton Area

Once Hofman arrived as far south as West Palm Beach, he joined William Linton and the other men who were to become the first settlers of Delray Beach. Apparently, Linton arranged for Frederick C. Voss, a settler in the Hypoluxo area who transported visitors by boat, to take the men in his launch across the long body of water known as Lake Worth. It was the only means of reaching the deserted wilderness to the south other than the mail boat, which made trips only once a week.

As the settlers proceeded south across Lake Worth, they were filled with awe by the pristine beauty of untouched tropical splendor. Snowy white egrets lifted their wings and took graceful flight in ingenuous wonder as the first white settlers disturbed their languor. Blue herons, oblivious to the encroaching boatload, rose only in protest as the men edged closer. Everywhere, there was incredible silence save the sputtering of the motor launch as it plied its way south across the long lake. The men remained speechless in the face of a frontier untouched and untamed. Tarpon and snook jumped from the sparkling water and disappeared beneath the sun-flecked rings of concentric circles they had created. The lake narrowed gradually, and a canopy of dark green vegetation enveloped the men as they glided silently down the waterway.

They disembarked at the south end of Lake Worth. The only means of traveling farther south was by barge. The men boarded the wide barge and slowly proceeded down the Florida Coast Line Canal begun in 1890 by a branch of Henry M. Flagler's empire, the Florida Coast Line Canal and Transportation Company. The canal had been dug for the purpose of transporting the materials needed to construct Flagler's railway south of West Palm Beach. The State of Florida gave the company 3,840 acres of land for each mile of canal constructed.

Carrying the handful of men, the barge embarked down the canal. Mangroves laced the sides of the canal with their intricate tracery of aerial roots and bowed their branches low over the waterway. Through openings between the roots, the men saw tiny fiddler crabs, which scampered down their holes into the wet bank as the barge bore on.

For hours the men were stupefied by the overwhelming loneliness and immensity of the landscape. To their left, the roar of the ocean surf could be heard at times, and to their right, muck land sucked up the gentle wake of the barge. In the distance, vast expanses of flatlands stretching in endless vistas were visible beyond the mangroves.

On board were William S. Linton, the leader; E. Burslem Thomson, a civil engineer; W. W. Blackmer, a Florida East Coast Railroad clerk; Frank W. Chapman, a former Michigan Central Railroad supply agent; and a number of farmers; including Fason Baker, Peter Luhrs, also known by his Anglicized name, Peter Lewis, Otto Schroeder, Kemp Burton, and Adolf Hofmann. Adolf later said that Alonzo Williams, a Mr. Fesenbecker, probably a misspelling of the name Carl Fesenberger, and a Mr. Wilson were also on the boat with him (Kingsbury, 70). Anglicizing or misspelling immigrant names was common among the early settlers. Adolf himself retained the German spelling of his surname for some time. Later, he used the second "n" sporadically and eventually dropped it.

At last the barge edged toward the left shore, a little north of a sizeable house, the only building in the area.

It was the House of Refuge No.3, otherwise known as the Orange Grove House of Refuge, built in 1876. It was one of five houses along the east coastline of Florida constructed by the United States Life Saving Service as places of refuge for shipwrecked sailors. Captain Stephen Andrews, the keeper of the house, heard their approach and ran out to meet them. As the men left the barge, they stepped onto the oozing muck bordering the canal and crossed a morass before climbing the large ridge of sand that supported the House of Refuge. Adolf stated that he and the others arrived on October 5, 1895.

House of Refuge No. 3, known as the Orange Grove House of Refuge, was built by the United States Life Saving Service in 1876 as a rescue station for shipwrecked sailors. (Courtesy of Delray Beach Historical Society)

They may have stayed overnight or longer in the Orange Grove House of Refuge as the guests of Stephen and Annie Andrews. Hofman said he went back to West Palm Beach for three weeks so he could stock up on needed supplies while the civil engineer was surveying and laying out the town. He wrote that two of his most necessary items, in addition to a tent, were a hand pump and enough pipeline to sink a well. Adolf and other settlers went back and forth to West Palm Beach on the mail boat several times. He said that when he returned to Linton, he and the other men lived in tents around the present area of Northeast Seventh Avenue and Northeast First Street for a few months. Hofman discovered he could obtain a supply of excellent drinking water by driving a pipe down only fifteen feet. The well and hand pump were essential to Adolf and Anna when they established their home site in 1895.

The Settlement of Linton

In order to secure the town site, William Linton had to make several land purchases. Linton purchased part of the town site from Simeon Brinson and John Herring, who had already made some shrewd land deals in the area. Their first clever move was to buy 160 acres from the State Board of Education for $1.25 an acre in 1895. Next, they sold a strip of this land 100 feet wide running right through the heart of the future town site as a right of way to the Jacksonville, St. Augustine and Indian River Railway Company for one dollar (Diggans, 1). Shortly thereafter, on September 9, 1895, the name was changed to the Florida East Coast Railway. The Dade County Official Deed Book "N" records that Brinson and Herring then sold the rest of their 160 acres to Linton for $30 an acre on October 14, 1895.

Moreover, Linton bought a large tract from A.F. Quimby, Clerk of the Circuit Court of Dade County, in 1895. Henry Sterling, one of the early settlers, said that in this transaction, Quimby sold one-half of Section 16 (320 acres) to Linton and in the deal gave the plot of land for a school in the proposed town (Kingsbury, 2).

Linton also bought a half section of land east of the canal from William and George Gleason. In addition, Linton bought land west of Swinton Avenue from the Model Land Company, a subsidiary of Flagler's Florida East Coast Railway (Kingsbury, 2).

As a result of these land purchases, Linton now had more than enough land for the site of the future town. The men worked tirelessly at establishing a settlement. E. Burslem Thomson, the civil engineer who came with the settlers in October 1895, began the laborious task of surveying the surrounding area and drawing a map of the

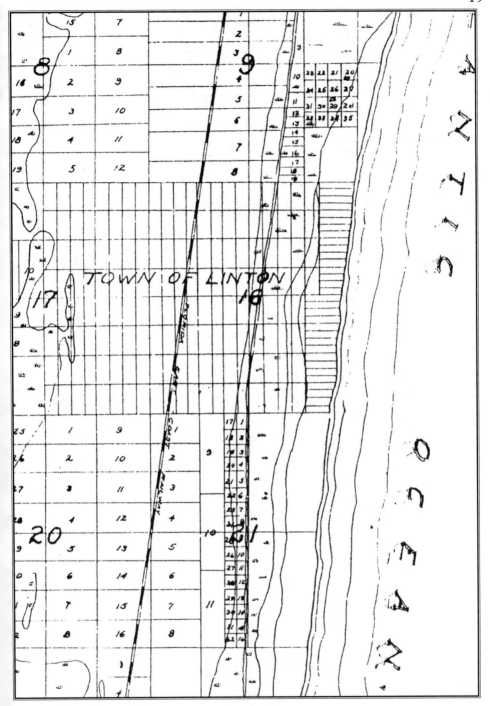

The original map of the Town of Linton was surveyed and drawn in October 1895 by E. Burslem Thomson, the engineer who came on the first barge with Linton and Hofman.

proposed town. In a few weeks, Thomson had the new town surveyed and plotted (Kingsbury, 21). The town was named Linton after its founder. The name was officially registered with the United States Post Office on October 18, 1895.

At first, Linton planned to lay out the town one and five-eighths of a mile south of today's Atlantic Avenue, but Captain Andrews convinced him to survey the main street at its present site by showing him the remains of an old rock wall and a large grove of sour orange trees and other tropical fruit that signified earlier settlement at that site. "The remains of an ancient rock wall surrounding about an acre of a wild orange grove were discovered. Just west of the orange grove was a natural waterway running north and south between the ocean ridge and the muck land" (Peebles, Interview with Adolf Hofman, 1937). Accordingly, Linton had Thomson run Atlantic Avenue parallel to this old rock wall. The original town of Linton was a mile from north to south and a mile and a half from east to west. It stretched from the ocean to Blackmer Avenue, which is today's Northwest Fifth Avenue, and extended four blocks north of Atlantic Avenue and four blocks south. The plat for the Town of Linton was recorded in the Dade County records on July 25, 1896.

Adolf spent several weeks reconnoitering the area in search of fertile soil and an elevated spot on which to build his house. He also searched for expansive acreage suitable for farming. Before him stretched acres and acres of saw palmetto and scrub brush infested with mosquitoes and choked with cabbage palms. Far to the west were clumps of pines and spruce trees anchored in sandy soil. From the old coastal ridge west of town, the land sloped down to the rich, muck soil by the canal. The view stretched on endlessly, offering land for the taking, and Adolf was eager to buy as much as he could afford. Quail and mourning doves roamed the quiet landscape unaware that civilization was soon to claim their domain.

After the town had been surveyed, Adolf moved his tent to an area north of the platted town limits, on the sixty acres that were to become his property. Here he homesteaded. His tent just east of Northeast Seventh Avenue and south of Sixth Street was situated thirty feet south of the spot where he built his first makeshift cabin. Anna and his daughter Annie arrived in Linton on December 28, 1895.

A lonesome sand road led to the beach in the Linton years. This is how much of Linton looked in 1895. (Courtesy of Delray Beach Historical Society)

*Two days after her arrival in the area,
Anna wrote her first letter home from Linton.*

Linton, December 30, 1895

Lieber Mother,

At last I am arrived in Florida after my long voyage from our dear fatherland to Nord-Amerika. I embarked from Le Havre on a French ship named *La Bourgogne* and arrived in the port of New York on December 23. All on board suffered from the high seas during the slow passage until we came to New York City. Much of my discomfort came from traveling with Annie who, as you know, is only three months old. So severely did I suffer from seasickness that Ursula and the other ladies on board had to care for Annie.

How fortunate I was to have cousins Phillip and Ursula make the journey with me to Amerika. As planned, they continued with me as far as St. Augustine to see me safely arrived in Florida. There we said our sad farewells, and they returned to New York and a new life of their own, knowing full well I must make my own life here with Adolf.

How kind it was of the Betz family, Germans from Stuttgart, to come from Boynton to meet me in St. Augustine. Without Karl Betz and his wife Mildred, I doubt if I should ever have found my way to West Palm Beach alone without speaking English. Mr. Betz arranged for a Mr. Voss to transport us across Lake Worth in his launch, but more to my surprise was the *last part of the journey by barge on a narrow canal.*

Along with my luggage, my steamer trunk could scarcely fit, strapped together across the barge, as the Betzes and I, holding Annie, stood up until we met our destination.

How alien was all the vegetation and how vast the land looked. There were dark, thick mangroves along the banks of the canal, sinking their long roots, into the murky water. Not far from the coastline, clusters of sea oats and brown grass clung to the wind-swept dunes. Plants with spikes, or pointed spears, called Spanish bayonets by Mr. Voss, grew in thick clumps. Everywhere I looked, the land lay flat on the horizon, stretching unbroken as far as I could see.

When we reached our destination at last, we were met by a Capt. Stephen Andrews. Adolf had to be called from the fields, for he was busy clearing the land. He was touched to see Annie for the first time. He was quite proud to hold her as his firstborn, even though his work clothes were stained and he was blackened from the sun and exhausted from labor. How burnt and blistered he was from months of difficult work. How tired he looked.

The Betzes returned to the barge and headed back to their farm in Boynton several miles north of Adolf's land. It is good to have fellow Deutschmen near so I will not feel too strange of tongue in this new land.

Our little house is only a makeshift cabin so far, but Adolf and a man named Mr. Wilson labored to finish the crude floor and roof in time for my arrival. Another man named Mr. Fessenberger, a fine carpenter, helped them as well. They also helped Adolf sink the pipeline for our hand pump. At night, we must soak burlap fertilizer bags in kerosene, then wring them out to drape across the windows to keep out hordes of mosquitoes.

Adolf pointed out that the little house sits on a hill. It is hardly a hill as we know it, yet more of an elevation of land that sweeps down to the canal and will keep us safe from flooding, he assures me. The hill is made of fine, white sand and is covered with low jagged-leafed brush the locals call palmetto. They use the roots as fuel for cooking over an open fire, if you can picture such a thing. Capt. Andrews taught Adolf and the other settlers how to use these roots for fuel. He also showed them how to get honey from the flowers of the saw palmetto.

Capt. Andrews also taught them how to make a smokeless cooking fire from the dry brackets, or "boots," of the cabbage palm, which bracket the tree like a thick trellis. The boot-jackets are the stalks of leaf fans that dry out and become brittle after the leaf fan has fallen. Around the house we have few trees save slash pines and several isolated clumps of cabbage palms. Everywhere, a fine redtop grass bows to the breezes sweeping over the newly cleared land.

I must hasten to post this letter while Mrs. Andrews, known as Annie, still gathers the mail for the few people living near the canal. Our little area was once called Zion because Annie gave that name to the post office she operated out of the House of Refuge until two years ago. She and her husband Stephen are known as the keepers of the House of Refuge, which is a shelter for shipwrecked sailors.

Adolf will take me across the canal on his own small barge, or lighter, as they call it, to greet the Andrews, who so befriended him and others when they arrived.

Annie's Zion—how much that name means to me. I think of Zion in Scripture, the City of God, "the promised land of milk and honey." How much I hope our little Zion will likewise blossom and bear good fruit. I pray that Zion will become my stronghold in this new and awe-inspiring wilderness. I must say farewell now, Mother. Adolf is here for me. I will write you often so I will not be homesick for you and the family in Erpfingen.

My greetings and love to all of you,
Anna

ANNA'S BACKGROUND AND EARLY LIFE

Anna also came from a farming community and a staunch Lutheran family. Anna Maria Dreher was born in the small village of Erpfingen, Germany, on April 1, 1874. The eldest of eight children, she was born to Karl Eduard Dreher and Bernhardine Margarete Bez. The Dreher family can be traced back to Johanes Dreher, born in 1626, while their roots in the village of Erpfingen, near the city of Reutlingen, date back to 1678. Generation followed generation working as farmers in this village located in southwest Germany in the Schwäbische Alb.

Erpfingen, Anna's birthplace, is a quiet village in southwest Germany.

As the eldest child, Anna cared for her younger brothers and sisters and shared many household and farmyard duties with her parents. After a prolonged and costly illness, her father died in 1892 at the age of forty-one, and the family struggled to maintain the Dreher farm. At the age of fourteen, Anna was sent to work as a maid in the Hofmann house in Mönchhof and continued working there for several years. While he was serving as an estate overseer, Adolf met Anna during his visits home. It was during these visits that they fell in love.

During his tenure as an estate supervisor in nearby Alteburg in 1894, Adolf planned to marry Anna, but Adolf's parents did not approve of the marriage, perhaps because of her impoverished family background. Farmers in those days emulated the marriage policies of the aristocracy. Both classes considered a prudently arranged marriage including inheritance and land a good avenue toward material security. Adolf's parents probably felt he should marry a girl from a farm comparable to theirs or preferably marry into a family with a large farm where there was no male heir.

As a result, Anna was sent away from the Hofmann farm in Mönchhof and was employed elsewhere. Nevertheless, after a quiet period of courtship, Adolf and Anna were married in August of 1894. The wedding remains somewhat of a mystery. Evidently, they had a civil wedding ceremony at the local guildhall in some small municipality away from the Mönchhof area, perhaps without the knowledge or approval of his family. This may explain Adolf's evasive or misleading answers in letters to his father about how many years Adolf had been married. Apparently, his father had no knowledge that Adolf was even married until years after Adolf's arrival in America. In fact, the family may never have realized that the woman Adolf married was Anna Dreher. At the end of several of his letters, Adolf signed his name and those of his children but never identified his wife's name.

Surviving in Early Linton

The task of surviving in this wilderness was excruciating. The men fought off wildcats, marauding boars, and hordes of mosquitoes so thick that they darkened the sky at times. Mosquitoes descended like black funnel clouds. The stings of the mosquitoes and other insects were so bad that the men had to bathe their skin with kerosene to soothe the bites and protect themselves against more attacks. The land was covered with palmetto roots that often grew six feet long and two or three feet deep into the sand. These had to be laboriously uprooted before building or farming could begin. While the men worked under the hot sun, huge horseflies attacked them day after day, inflicting painful, penetrating bites. Everywhere possums and polecats foraged for food. The exhausted workers had to ward off rattlesnakes, moccasins, raccoons, and wild boars. Rattlesnakes and panthers often lurked in the clumps of palmettos the men had to dig up. The panthers feverishly scratched the base of tree trunks until the bark was in shreds. Bears came out of the woods at night to prowl the beach for food.

"It was the hardihood and the fortitude of those early settlers that helped make Delray Beach what it is today. The town was built on a solid foundation of people who knew what privation was and were willing to work for their ideal" (Britt, *Delray Beach Journal*, Feb. 3, 1949).

Although the original settlers struggled to survive and establish roots in this rugged, hostile land, many of them eventually left the area. Otto Schroeder, who was single and lived in a shack down by the canal, purchased twenty acres. He stayed as long as ten years. Even though Mr. Wilson continued to live in a tent for six

The original settlers labored endlessly to carve a town out of the hostile wilderness.

months, he later left for Miami. Peter Luhrs, a German who spoke very good English, purchased twenty and a half acres north of Adolf's land and with Wilson's help built the first house in town. It was a fairly good one-story house, which had three rooms, and was nestled close to the canal (Kingsbury, 69). Luhrs remained in Linton only a short time, from October of 1895 to May of 1896, when he went to West Palm Beach. Another of the original settlers, Carl Fesenberger, eventually returned to Germany. Yet the lure of land and added adventure meant everything to Adolf, and he had come to stay.

Adolf's progress in Linton was interrupted by family news that brought mixed emotions.

Linton, January 6, 1896

Dear Father, Brothers, and Sisters,

First, let me tell you in what kind of turmoil I was recently, having received on Nov. 20 the following telegram: "Jerseyville, Nov. 15, 1895. Father died this morning at 9 o'clock. Signed: John and George Schwarz."

Upon reading this telegram, I thought that you, my dear father, had died and that my brothers and sisters—perhaps not knowing my address—had sent a wire to Uncle and asked him to send a wire to me in turn. At last I got a letter from Uncle's friend who is also his partner and the secretary at the electrical company, telling me that Uncle had died on Nov. 15.

He wrote me that Uncle had left a will and that his estate is estimated to amount to $37,000. He left legacies to his children and willed the remainder of his estate to his sister [Adolf's deceased mother] or her children. He wrote that each of us heirs might receive $4,000 to 5,000. He further wrote that I should come to Jerseyville in early February with full power of attorney from you, for it would be much better if I were there in person. What is your opinion, should I go there or not?

I am not particularly eager to go. First, it will be costly—at least $90 for the round trip, the distance being about two thousand miles, and second, my business here doesn't permit so long an absence. I asked a lawyer in West Palm Beach if my going to Jerseyville is really necessary. He said it would be better if one of the heirs were there, but not urgently necessary, since we would have to have a lawyer present whether or not I go.

Things go well with me in Florida. I am always in good health—thank God—even though I have been through lots of difficulties. As the old saying goes, "He who wants to walk under palms must first suffer from insect bites," and I have heavily suffered those. But things are getting better and better. When I first arrived in Linton, there were only two tents in which the engineers lived, but now there are more than one hundred tents, two general stores, two bakeries, and about thirty houses are being built. A compatriot of mine, also from Germany, Peter Luhrs, built the first house, and I built the second, which is almost near completion.

The railroad bed now passes through here, and roads are being built, so that there is quite some life going on. I received the money from home just in good time. If I had received it only one week later than I did, I could no longer have made a down payment on any land between the canal and the railroad, or would have had to pay twice as much.

Perhaps I shall have to go to Jerseyville to attend to the estate matters.

Regards and greetings,
Yours, Adolf

Early Mail Service

Mail delivery had a long and colorful history in the Linton area. Before 1885 an occasional postman carried soldiers' mail along the beach at random intervals. In the 1850s, during the Third Seminole War, "Long John" Holman carried the mail from St. Augustine to Biscayne Bay, hiding at night in caves along the coast. Such caves once existed just north of Linton, located behind the ocean ridge near today's Briny Breezes. Holman used these caves as a stopover. "Long John" Holman also served as a mail carrier in the area during the Civil War.

In 1885 the federal government contracted for mail carriers along the South Florida coast. These new government carriers had to be men who were eager for adventure and who did not mind facing danger and getting wet. With their shoes draped around their necks and rolled-up pants legs, they walked along the shoreline for three days to carry the mail from Juno-Palm Beach to Hypoluxo Island, then to Lemon City, and finally to the Miami River. The journey back took another three days. The route was fifty-six miles by small sailboats and rowboats and eighty miles on foot along the beach.

The first "barefoot mailman" was Edwin R. Bradley. He stayed overnight in the Orange Grove House of Refuge, which became the custom for the other mailmen. The Orange Grove House of Refuge was known for the warm hospitality shown by its keepers, Stephen and Annie Andrews. Its upstairs loft had a large sleeping area with cots, but at times the mailmen enjoyed sleeping on the wide veranda downstairs, which was open to the brisk ocean breezes.

The most famous of these letter carriers was James Edward Hamilton, who came to be known in history as the Barefoot Mailman. On October 10, 1887, Ed Hamilton mysteriously vanished while trying to swim across the Hillsborough Inlet on his southern journey. Someone had removed the mailman's boat he kept hidden along the banks in order to cross the inlet. Apparently, Hamilton died while trying to swim across the inlet to retrieve his boat. A search party found his canvas haversack containing the mail pouch and his trousers and shirt hanging on a tree where he usually kept his boat. The cause of his death is still a topic of debate. Some historians speculate that sharks attacked him, but others state that stormy weather that season had washed alligators eastward into the inlet. Ed Hamilton spent his last night on earth at the Orange Grove House of Refuge.

Annie Andrews ran the Zion post office out of the Orange Grove House of Refuge from 1885 to 1893. Several other men served as beachfront carriers until 1893, when a stagecoach route was established and the use of barefoot mailmen was discontinued. The Biscayne Bay Stage ran from Lantana to Lemon City. In addition to the stagecoach, a mail boat from West Palm Beach made weekly trips down the canal. Shortly after Linton was founded, Frank Chapman was appointed the first Postmaster of Linton in 1895.

Linton, January 10, 1896

Dear Mother,

 While Annie sleeps beside me, I must hurry and write you about my life in Linton, for so the settlers named our town last year to honor Mr. Linton. Yet I fear the proud name of Zion, which welcomed me warmly as a stranger, may now be lost forever. I would much prefer to use the old post office at Zion.
 For it is here near the House of Zion, the Orange Grove House of Refuge, that I write you today. This morning Adolf saw me to his lighter on the canal bank of our property for fear I should encounter the razorback boars that sometimes ravage the farms as cruelly as they did in November. As he pulled the chain attached to the barge, the heavy, submerged weight linked to the chain rose above the water, and with Annie in my arms, we moved slowly across the narrow canal.
 Capt. Andrews and his wife Annie met me on the other side, and together we edged our way through the dense thicket of mangroves. They are peculiar trees with air-borne roots that sink themselves into the water and muck of the canal. At length, we emerged from the tangle and proceeded to cross a wide morass choked with sawgrass, furiously fighting off the droves of mosquitoes that attacked us from every side.
 We proceeded to climb a steep ridge of dry sand rising above the muck land. Our shoes shuffled and slipped in the sand of the high ridge as we followed the trail to the House of Refuge. Everywhere, billowy

sea oats bowed by the ocean wind, nodded busily as we made our way across the soft sand, at times pale gold, at times pale tan beneath the shafts of sunlight. I think I shall never tire of so vast an ocean and so wide an expanse. Now I know why Adolf needed to make his adventure here to this boundless land, to stretch his arms and reach out as far as he could to realize his dreams.

We walked some paces to the south past the House of Refuge. Capt. Andrews, for so he is called, had in mind to show me the remains of a rock wall, which lay in ruins ahead of us to the south. Its builders, whoever they were, abandoned it countless years ago. Such strange stones—I ran my hand across the rough, uneven surface and was perplexed to find small crumbling shells embedded in each hewn square of rock that Capt. Andrews said is called coquina. He told me that Mr. Linton and Mr. Thomson laid out the main street of town just to the north of this wall, a sturdy remnant of some ancient settlers long before us. How mysterious to find these ruins from long ago. I wonder what became of the people who once walked these shores.

Behind the rock wall stretched what seemed to me an arbor, a large grove of trees laden with fruit. Capt. Andrews explained that he had urged Mr. Linton to settle at this spot without traveling farther south, for surely the orange trees and other fruit trees showed that frost would never come this far. He walked me to the wild sour orange trees, for those the House of Refuge is named, while telling me that ancient people, Spanish settlers, some think, planted them and built the wall that surrounds them years ago. Others claim the grove and wall are from fugitive Minorcans who fled from New Smyrna, Florida. Some people think wandering Indians might have planted the seeds many years ago. There seem as many as sixty to seventy trees laid out in some orderly pattern, set generally in rows, enclosed by the ruins of the wall. This leads me to favor the idea that Spanish settlers, sent with a land grant by their king, planted them on purpose, built the wall, and intended to start a permanent colony here. How mysterious it is that only these ruins remain to tell us we are not the first to settle here from far away.

Here the Andrews left me to write my letter in this sacred grove in Zion. One of the orange trees bears the name and date, "Charley Moore—1878" carved on its trunk. I wonder what fate befell him in this wild and windswept land. Here my Annie sleeps soundly as I write to you, sitting beneath the ripening oranges. How peaceful and quiet is the air. The gnarled old branches bear much fruit and shade me from the sun that hovers above the horizon to the south. These trees in Zion "bring forth fruit in their season" just as Scripture promises.

How I love to write to you, dear Mother, for I am often homesick, and it makes me feel as if you are here beside me sharing these experiences. Now I must close for Annie is stirring and much work awaits me across the canal.

Your loving daughter,
Anna

Adolf's Acquisition of Land

In contrast to the other original settlers, Adolf Hofman had come to stay. Led on by his determination and his dreams, Hofman regarded the acquisition and use of land as a major factor in his life in Delray Beach. His initial interest in South Florida was in part motivated by his desire to buy as much land as possible with the money he had.

Acres and acres of available land stretched for miles to the north, south, and west, waiting to be claimed and cultivated. Tall slash pines and southern spruce dominated the horizon of the flatlands. The high coastal ridge undulated in contours of dry soil and white sugar sand.

William Linton offered a five-acre tract of land in town to each of the men in his party, and Adolf was the first to purchase one of these tracts shortly after his arrival (Keen, *Delray Beach News*, Oct. 4, 1940). Experiencing financial difficulties, however, Linton defaulted on his own land payments in 1898, a year after he left town for good. Linton's creditors began to foreclose on his mortgages.

As a result of the foreclosures, Hofman, who had paid Linton in full for his land, had to pay for his own five acres once again. He was one of the few men to do so and one of the few original settlers to remain in Linton as a permanent resident. No doubt his determination, German fortitude, and sense of destiny drove him on. Hofman now had five acres in town and claim to sixty acres north of town. Adolf may not have fully realized in 1895 that he was just in advance of the most revolutionary force in South Florida's history, the empire of Henry M. Flagler, whose railway would sweep south, open the sleepy frontier, and change Florida forever.

Hofman said that when he arrived in 1895, the Florida East Coast Railway had finished the grading as far as Linton, but no railroad ties or rails had been laid south of West Palm Beach (Kingsbury, 67). Flagler was interested in selling land to immigrants and industrious families who, in turn, would populate new settlements strung along his ever-advancing railway and raise crops for his trains to transport to market.

The Hofman home was a two-story frame structure built in February 1896. Adolf's makeshift cabin built in 1895 is located on the left. Left to right: Clara, Anna, Annie, and Adolf in 1902.

Adolf and Anna continued to occupy their land north of town. In February of 1896, they moved into their two-story home, where they continued to live the rest of their lives.

Linton, February 2, 1896

Dear Mother,

    At last our two-story house is finished and there is so much to tell you. As you may recall, our little cabin rests upon a hill, as does this house. Mr. Hoenes, the builder, was careful to situate it facing east to capture the sea breezes. Mr. Fesenberger once again did all the carpentry, and Mr. Wilson worked along with him. We were fortunate to have good lumber brought in by train now that the freight trains run as far as West Palm Beach. As of yet, the town has not extended any road in our direction since Adolf's land is north of the village. We have only a dirt trail that leads to the house through the palmettos. There is a good clearing to help ward off the mosquitoes and horseflies.

    The white sand in the clearing is covered with redtop grass and sandspurs. I am always entertained by small wildflowers, which dance daily in the sandy yard. Soon we will plant sprouted coconuts and guava trees near the house to provide some shade during the hot summers. Adolf has already planted a new type of fruit tree, known as a turpentine mango tree, the fruit of which is tart and has a golden, stringy pulp.

Our house is a wood frame, two-story structure having a steep pitched roof bearing wood shingles. We also have fanciful, rounded, clapboard shingles on the front gables and eaves and a long, wide front porch to welcome guests and protect us from sun and rain. Already I have put the porch to good use. On the porch beams I've hung clusters of palmetto berries to dry, for I am told they make a fine tonic.

I am most pleased with the balcony and open porch on the second story. From there we overlook the canal in the distance, and if I stretch high enough on my toes, I can catch a glimpse of the ocean when the breakers are driven by the wind. Two doors built side by side lead from the upstairs hall to this open porch. These are most necessary in this hot climate, for when both are opened, plentiful breezes sweep through the upper floor and down the stairway. Mr. Hoenes assures us that the heat will rise and escape through the attic windows placed in the steeply pitched roof. The sash windows with their weights and cord pulleys open from both top and bottom to increase the circulation.

Imagine, I have a room with a large tub for bathing right next to our bedroom upstairs. Annie's room is also upstairs to one side, and ours is to the other side of the stairs, the northeast corner of the house. From the north window we can see the pump and cistern, and from the east window we can see the property slope down to the canal and Adolf's small lighter. At night the salted sea air, fanned by the ocean breezes, seeps into the room.

What pleases me most is our front door, for it welcomes guests warmly. Four etched glass panels form the top half of the door and cast a filtered glow as if the glass is frosted when the sun shines through it in early morning. More glorious is a doorknob of great dignity, for the outside knob is a glossy brown enamel, and the inside knob is faceted glass, cut and beveled like an enormous jewel. It refracts the light from the glowing glass door panels etched to look like lace.

Next to the front door I keep my brush broom, which I made from crisp, dry palmetto fans by tying twine around their long stems to form a handle. Everyone coming through the door must first have the mosquitoes brushed off them. I also use my palmetto broom for sweeping the front porch clean each day.

Our little makeshift cabin with its stovepipe will serve me well for the kitchen and eating area since it is located right behind our two-story house. Adolf has reminded Mr. Hoenes that he has yet to put up a lightning rod at each end of the roof on our new house. Capt. Andrews warns us that summer storms bring with them severe lightning strikes.

The other night, after Annie was asleep, Adolf took me to the parlor and unrolled a copy of the survey map of Linton drawn by Mr. Thomson. We strained to see the map by the faint glow of the kerosene lamp. Adolf pointed out the five-acre tract he bought from Mr. Linton. As his finger continued to sweep across the map, he pointed to more land he wanted to buy, entire blocks to claim as his own, and his voice grew with excitement over all that we could have in this new wilderness.

I must close now, Mother, because I want to look through the Montgomery Ward catalog at Mr. Sterling's commissary and order a table and chairs as well as four kerosene lamps for the new house.

Your loving daughter,
Anna

Even though uncertainties plagued him in the early years, Adolf struggled to remain positive.

Linton, March 4, 1896

Dear Brother Fritz,

I received your letters and also the money that Father sent. I resolved to go to Jerseyville and have only just returned. I left there on February 3, and I am glad now that I was there even though the trip cost me a good deal of money. Our case involving the Schwarz inheritance is a very complicated matter and will no doubt take a long time to settle. The attorney in Jerseyville told me it would be advantageous if one of the heirs remained present, because otherwise the lawyers would do just as they please. But by staying longer, I would have incurred more losses at my farm than the possible financial gains from the inheritance money. Those four weeks I spent there cost me several hundred dollars in crop damage. I have to make up for this now with increased effort and work hours.

If I had foreseen matters and if I had been able to invest about $2,500 in my farm, then I could be a rich man by now, but that kind of knowledge always comes too late. But who could have known to invest so much when failure appeared just as likely. I believe that farming in Linton will turn out profitable, but it takes lots of money before you can do anything at all. It's hard to believe what means are necessary just to buy the most urgent things in this wilderness.

Had I bought my farmland just one month earlier and planted my fields earlier, I could have reaped a net profit of $1,000. Prices of produce are abnormally high because everything froze in California and in the southern states, and even just north of Linton. We also had small losses from frost, but just a little south of Linton, nothing froze.

Whoever can ship vegetables right now has made his fortune. My harvesting time will be in late April, and I hope to earn a net profit of $500 to $600 even then. Right now, I have fine potatoes, lettuce, beets, cabbage, radishes, and other vegetables. But the amount planted is still so small that I need most of it for my family.

The Model Land Company grants a 10 percent discount if you pay them before June 1; otherwise, they charge 6 percent interest. So therefore, I ask you to write me how much money our Father will be able to send me, in case I would pay for my land immediately, provided that my harvest turns out good. I planted one acre of Paradise apples, one acre of tomatoes, one acre of beans, one acre of cabbage, one acre of potatoes, and about one-quarter acre of other vegetables. If all goes well, I should reap a good harvest late in April.

       With the best regards and greetings,
              Your brother,
                  Adolf

Linton, April 2, 1896

Dear Mother,

 I took to my garden this morning while Adolf was out in the north fields clearing off scrub brush and palmetto from the last section of our land.
 The sun is beating with full force on the garden, and as long as I can keep the crows and wild rabbits away, we should have plenty to eat. The rabbits devour everything they can find, even the tender green shoots of the coconut palms as soon as they begin to sprout. But the rabbits are little to worry about when compared to our other dangers. We must also always be on guard against the razorback hogs that are drawn to the garden. They forage for food everywhere with their fierce, long snouts and short hocks. With their backs arched and their snouts forever buried in the ground, they make no distinction between eating rats, snakes, hares, or vegetation. And our garden proves an easy treat for them.
 The other grave danger Adolf always warns me about are the snakes that lie hidden everywhere, particularly the venomous rattlesnakes. They are known to hide in the fields and are on the move since settlers have begun to build in town. Clumps of palmettos are their favorite hiding place. I must also be forever on guard against the cottonmouth moccasins, which lurk down by the canal and resemble the gray mud of the trail leading to the canal.
 Today the garden is peaceful and partially shaded by the tall plants surrounding it. Adolf transplanted a number of wild pawpaws from the beach area

when he started our garden last year near the pump area. All of them prospered along with the wild coffee plants he uprooted from the beach hammocks. Capt. Andrews showed us how to grind the coffee beans and brew them together with charred sweet potatoes. We must first cut the sweet potatoes into chunks and bake them until they are dark brown and crisp. Then we grind them in the coffee mill along with our wild coffee beans and brew the mixture. It makes for a strong, rich brew that Adolf likes quite well. And the sweet potatoes we have growing everywhere, for they flourish with little or no care as do the morning glories and periwinkles, which thrive in the sandy soil surrounding the house.

Sweet potatoes and greens make a fine meal, and sometimes I serve them with squirrel stew. Capt. Andrews also showed Adolf how to cut the heart out of a cabbage palm. The palm heart yields a clean, white meat somewhat like a cabbage. I cook it by first frying some cubes of salt pork, throwing in some sliced palm cabbage, or swamp cabbage as we call it, and steaming it good and long. Capt. Andrews also taught us how to eat the waxy flowers of Spanish bayonets by dipping them in batter and frying them. He also roasts the Yucca fruit over an open fire once he removes the hard seeds.

A breeze from the canal fans me as I work in the garden gathering beans and eggplant. It is a quiet, still morning save for the chanters. Not more than several hundred yards away, over by the railroad grading, the voices of the workmen are chanting in unison. The head chanter leads them with a steady beat. The mockingbirds are making great sport of trying to join the melody as the chanter calls out the words to the workmen laying the ties and rails. Each day they move a little farther south to Linton, and people say that it won't be long before we can all ship our produce north by rail. I wonder if Adolf knew he was settling in the shadow of Flagler's empire when he first chose this site last year. I can hear the workers repeating the rhythmic chants over and over again, and I can see the handcar travel back and forth every once in a while over the newly laid rails. Those mockingbirds are enjoying such company, too.

Farther to the north, I can see smoke rising from the ground. Adolf is torching the last of the palmetto scrub, for so he does to help clear the rest of our land. He digs trenches around the field to contain the fire. Then he drags a torch of dried palmetto fans through the field, across the underbrush, until everything becomes a blazing sheet of flames. Most of the wildlife escapes safely, but hundreds of rattlers are consumed in the fire. What is left are charred stumps and smoking palmetto roots that have to be pulled from the ground to clear it for plowing. Yet the torching does its job in clearing the brush and wildlife, and Adolf will be happy once all our land has been cleared for planting.

I can still hear the chanters in the distance. Yet the approaching railroad seems indifferent to the chanters, or the mockingbirds, or the settlers. I wonder how it will change all our lives.

Give my warmest greetings to all the relatives. Remember me in your thoughts.

Your loving daughter,
Anna

Linton, April 29, 1896

Dear Mother,

 Adolf is pleased that his brother Gottlieb Friedrich is visiting us all the way from Stuttgart. Fritz, as Adolf calls him, has journeyed to America to help resolve matters concerning the estate of their late uncle, John Schwarz. The settling of their rightful inheritance still lingers in the courts. After spending some time in the old city of St. Augustine, Fritz boarded the train and arrived in Linton several days ago.

 He has yet to adjust to the heat and the hordes of insects. We keep a small smudge fire going in front of the porch, and I brush everyone off with my palmetto broom before they enter the house. Still we are bitten by the mosquitoes, which are more plentiful than usual at this time of year. Every afternoon, black thunderheads gather on the western horizon in the Glades and carry the torrential rainstorms that deluge us day after day. The morass down by the canal is so saturated that water stands for days, breeding even more mosquitoes and other insects.

 This morning, to beat the afternoon thunderstorms, Adolf took Fritz across the canal, where they headed north along the coast. After several miles of walking, Adolf located the caves he wanted to show Fritz. Legend has it that the caves north of Linton were once the site of buried pirate treasure hidden beneath the large slab of stone on the side of the opening. So far none has ever been discovered.

 On the low dunes near the coast, Adolf showed Fritz turtle nests that contained hundreds of turtle eggs. They wanted to save the adventure of digging up the eggs for another time. On the other side of the dunes, Adolf used his machete to cut off a spray of black berries from a cabbage palm so Fritz could sample a taste. Even though he managed to eat a few, right down to the small seed inside, Fritz found the pungent berries somewhat bitter.

    They walked back across the wide sand ridge to capture the needed relief brought by the trade winds, which kept away the sand fleas, or little "no-see-ums" as they are called. They crossed the morass and worked their way through the mangrove thicket.

    Fighting off mosquitoes, they edged their way to the narrow canal crossing where an alligator lay partly submerged in the water, unaware of their approach. Excited by his first sight of the reptile, Fritz reached for Adolf's rifle and shot the gator in the neck. This caused the gator to jerk and twist sideways, exposing its underbelly. Fritz shot again and again at the soft underbelly, and the gator writhed back and forth in spasms of agony until, at last, it lay lifeless in the mud. Fritz insisted on dragging the alligator to our barn, where he and Adolf skinned it and fed the meat to the chickens. With a pair of pliers, Fritz yanked out some of the gator's teeth to save as keepsakes of his trip. Fritz also plans to take the hide with him to Germany when he returns.

    That night I treated Fritz to pawpaws for dessert, and it took him some time to get used to the sweet spongy flesh. Good thing for him that the wild persimmons, which ripen in August, were not yet ready. It's too bad the mangoes are not ripe yet, for I think Fritz would enjoy their tart and fibrous meat. I use the dried stringy seed of the turpentine mango to make little hairy animal toys for Annie to play with.

When the sun had finally set, we sat in the wide swing on the front porch, trying to catch a breath of air in the humid night. Adolf walked down the steps and stirred up the smudge fire. Then he brought a smudge bucket right up on the porch to help keep the mosquitoes away. There we sat for a long time, watching the heat lightning flash in the distance. Each sudden flash outlined enormous clouds, which quivered in shades of pearl and opal.

We talked of our fatherland and memories of home. I wonder whether or not Fritz will reveal my identity to his father. He has never inquired about my name or background, and Adolf's father, absent at our wedding, thinks Adolf is safely married to some woman from Alteburg. His father little thought Adolf had gone ahead and married the very woman they had disapproved of in Mönchhof. Yet has it made any difference? Here we are sitting on the far fringe of the continent, and Adolf's family is awakening to a new day on the other side of the ocean. Adolf has his land and the freedom to realize whatever he dreams, and I have followed him here in love and devotion, content with my family and home. What would we have had in the fatherland but disapproval and rejection? Here we have the endless horizon, the wild freedom of the sea, and a sky full of stars that judge us not.

From your loving daughter,
Anna

The Hofman Homestead

Adolf was pleased with the site he had homesteaded in 1895. His purchase of this homestead involved considerable risk taking and shrewd bargaining—especially for an immigrant still learning how to speak English. After cleverly negotiating the price with the Model Land Company, Adolf purchased the sixty acres in 1896 and received Deed No. 1 from the Model Land Company free and clear in June of 1896.

This land was the foothold that secured him to the area and afforded him opportunities for expansion. The sixty acres comprised all of Lot 7, Section 9, in Township 46 South, Range 43 East, and stretched from Swinton Avenue to the canal. It ran approximately 750 feet from Northeast Seventh Street to Northeast Fifth Street. This included the area where he pitched his tent, sank his well, built his cabin and his two-story house, all of which were located just east of Northeast Seventh Avenue and south of Northeast Sixth Street.

Although north of Linton's city limits, the location of the Hofman homestead was ideally situated for farming and shipping. Cutting through his land was the Florida East Coast Railway, which claimed rights to fifty feet of land on either side of the railroad. Pushing south to Linton in 1896, the railroad tracks ran diagonally straight through the heart of Hofman's acreage and promised an accessible and rapid means of shipping his produce from Linton to northern markets.

Right: Adolf kept Deed No.1 from the Model Land Company, the deed to his sixty-acre homestead, locked in a safe hidden at home beneath the pantry floor along with his other deeds and documents.

DEED No. 1

THIS INDENTURE, made this ninth day of June, in the year of our Lord One thousand eight hundred and ninety-six A.D.1896, between the MODEL LAND COMPANY, a corpor[ation of] the State of Florida, party of the first [part, and ...] the County of Dade and State [of Florida ...]

W[HEREAS,] the [...] [f]irst part, for and in consider[ation of ...] [dol]lars, to it in hand paid by the [...] the ensealing and delivery [...] is hereby acknowledged, hath [...] [conve]yed and confirmed, and by th[ese presents does ... r]elease, convey and confirm un[to ...] his heirs and assigns, all that [...] [ly]ing and being in the County of D[ade ...] [des]cribed as follows:

Lot number [...] [Sec]tion Nine (9) in Township [... Range forty-th]ree (43) East, containing Si[...] [an]d reserving the right of w[ay ...] [a]cross the same, being a strip [of land ...] [fif]ty feet in width on each si[de ...] of said Railway as now c[onstructed].

Together with [...] [h]ereditaments and appurtenances [...] [a]nywise appertaining.

TO HAVE AND TO H[OLD the said premises and app]urten- ances, and every part [thereof, unto the said party of the se]cond part his heirs and assigns [...]

And the said [party of the] first part and its successors, the said premises and every part thereof, unto the said party of the second part his heirs and assigns, against it, the said party of the first part, and its successors, and all and every other person

---

Model Land Company
to
Adolf Hofmann

Dated June 9th 1896

STATE OF FLORIDA,
DADE COUNTY.
This instrument was filed for record
this 13 day of June 1896
[...] Book [...] on Page 296
of Deeds
[...]
A H Quimby

Rec Fee # 1.20

Linton, June 5, 1896

My Dear Father,

I received those 4,000 Deutsche Marks, for which I got $940 paid out four weeks ago. I would have notified you at once that I received it, but I wasn't quite sure then in which manner it would be best to put the money to use.

I considered keeping it as working capital for starting a pineapple plantation, but since I did not yet own the land, I decided not to invest it in this project, but rather to pay cash for my land first. But to do this, the money was not quite sufficient since I owed $1,500, which if I paid cash immediately, I would get a 12 percent discount, leaving $1,300. But I had only $1,150 altogether, namely those $940 from your 4,000 marks, $100 in the bank from your last money transfer, and another $110 from selling potatoes and beans. So what was I to do?

So I proposed to the Model Land Company that if they gave me a 24 percent discount on the price of the land, I would pay at once, if not, I would go elsewhere and buy my land there. I led them to believe that when brother Fritz was here we had looked at land just as good as that of the Company, which we could buy at $15 an acre, and that my brother only returned to Germany in order to get more people here who would buy the land together with us.

This was like setting a fire at the Company. Mr. Linton and the general agent came to see me and immediately offered a 20 percent discount, but I insisted on 24 percent, and they gave me that, too, so that finally I had to pay only $1,140, leaving me now merely $10. The Company asked me would I notify my brother at once that for each man who comes here and buys land on account of his recommendation, the Company will give him $20. The general agent said that if I were to sell land at $25 per acre in cash, he would give me 24 percent of the proceeds. Of course I would have to pass on 12 percent discount to the buyers, otherwise they would buy directly from the Company.

Thus, if a man were to buy forty acres, I would earn $120. If you could recruit five to ten such buyers for me, I could have a flourishing business here. Those people who don't wish to pay immediately are granted seven years before their payment is due, but they have to pay 8 percent interest during that time.

If perhaps Friedrich in Oberroth [Adolf's brother-in-law who ran a general store] would be inclined to take on an agency, then I could have the general agent send him the various papers required. I would pay him a commission of ten dollars for each man who buys land from this Company, but better not tell him I was offered a $20 commission.

But only people with at least some money should be sent over, because without money you cannot get anything going here, just as it is in Germany. The Model Land Company still has over two million acres to sell, and they are pushing to sell the land as quickly as possible because they have already started to build a canal west of here on the fresh water lake.

Last week, a pastor from Sweden was here and bought thirty thousand acres near Fort Lauderdale for his countrymen. Moreover, the day before yesterday, a farm manager from Holland came here to evaluate land. He leaves today and plans to come back with 200 to 300 families from there.

Of the Germans here, half of them will have to leave again since they can't support themselves. First, they don't want to work as hard as required, and second, they have no money. The two Swabians here make good progress; however, I got my land cheaper than they, for they paid $1,000 dollars for twelve acres and I got sixty acres for $1,140.

The pineapple farmers earn big money this year. That forty-acre farm of pineapple fields I told you about is shipping a railroad car full of pineapples each day and gets twenty-five to fifty cents apiece on the average. Also the pineapple plantation Fritz and I visited is said to bring in good money as well. In addition, those vegetable farmers of Hypoluxo have made good profits. There are some in Linton who made over $1,000. For instance, my neighbor across the canal earned $1,400. If only I could have shipped my produce two weeks earlier, I could have gotten three times as much as right now. There can be no doubt that things will work out well here in due time.

Best wishes and greetings,
Yours, Adolf

Linton, June 9, 1896

Dear Mother,

    Today I am heading for the fields since Adolf needs me with him now that the okra is ready to be picked. Annie must come with me because there are no neighbors nearby to watch her except the Betzes, who live some three miles away in Boynton, and the Mullers, who live near us, but they also have their fields and much work to do.
    Fortunately, I am conditioned for hard work from the farm in Erpfingen. Remember when father died and the boys were young and you and I struggled to maintain the properties? We were hardened in no time from the constant labor. How God equips us for what we need to do. I thank God I am sturdy. For so it was with Adolf and the hard work he had at his home place in Mönchhof with much land to till. Yet he did not weary—so keen was his interest in growing things.
    You and I know the hardships of working old land, but Adolf knows how to tame this new, wild landscape surrounding us, and, what is more, he is eager about it at all times. Adolf paid for our sixty acres and got the deed. Our land stretches far beyond our house in every direction and continues down to the canal. We own land across the railroad tracks farther than I can see.
    Today I am working in the okra field, which slopes from our hill to the canal. Adolf was wise to place okra there, for thus the drainage is good and no flood can engulf the plants since the water drains

into the canal. Adolf also planted rows of horse banana palms to absorb any flow of water from the west and to form a windbreak for the beans. Here in Linton, we have a constant battle against the crows and cutworms, and what is worse, wild raccoons and rats gnaw at the vegetables endlessly. The possums and raccoons even eat the shiny black fruit of the palmettos, which grow everywhere.

A most unexpected and terrible frost on February 18 ruined some of our crops and drove many people out of town. They had been promised good crops and the absence of frost by Mr. Linton and were not prepared to cope with the hard freeze that came our way. Devastated by the loss of all their crops, many disillusioned settlers gave up and left town.

At first, we also mourned for our losses and our souls were heavy. Yet we did not despair, for as Adolf noted, the ground itself was not actually frozen and the cold spell did not last. Of course the delicate plants snapped, unable to bear the frost. Many plants withered or broke in two from the thin layer of ice that encased them during that frigid night. At least we have knowledge of farming and experience with failure, while some settlers came here with little or no farming experience at all.

As the temperatures dropped lower and lower that night, Adolf built small fires in the fields, feeding them green palmetto leaves to increase the smoke. He hoped to create a smudge that would cover the fields and stave off the frost. The smoke hovered about the ground and slowly drifted over the rows of beans and eggplant and tomatoes. The smoke and a stiff breeze from the ocean just before dawn kept some of our crops from freezing. Yes, we lost patches of crops, but we were determined to plant again and wait for the land to produce. For such is nature. Some plants survive—others wilt and perish—so the cycle goes. So it is with us here in Linton. Already some have left in bitter disappointment and despair, yet some, like us, stay and endure. For endurance is the way of a true farmer, and we are young and determined to remain on our good land.

Sturdy though I am, I am still victim of the flying insects that eagerly attack me. They are constant and relentless, and I must cover Annie's basket with cheesecloth netting to shield her from their vicious attacks. Always I carry with me a type of fan I have fashioned from dried palmetto fronds by wrapping cord around their stems. I must swish away deer flies, sucking horseflies, and mosquitoes. You cannot imagine, Mother, how ferocious and ever-present these insects are.

And the sun in Florida is equally unmerciful at this time of year. Our clothes are wet and cling heavily all day long and well into the night from the high humidity. The sun is known to actually burn and blister the skin if one is not careful to wear a wide-brimmed hat and keep the long sleeves buttoned.

Thus are our days in the fields, but I am content to follow Adolf and feel a part of this new adventure and the rich soil that surrounds us.

> Love to all at home,
> Anna

As a result of Flagler's newly opened railroad extension, Miami sprang into a boom town that beckoned builders and opportunists. In contrast, Linton remained a quiet community characterized by hardworking farmers and shopkeepers.

The old Florida East Coast Railway station, built in 1896, was the busy hub of activity for packers, shippers, and passengers.
(Courtesy of Delray Beach Historical Society)

Linton, July 9, 1896

Dear Father,

 In Linton there is much activity going on now that the railway goes through town. At present, there is very heavy traffic with the trains. People all flock from the North to Miami and think all they have to do is to shake the money from the trees. Supposedly, more than one hundred houses are reported to be going up there each week. Every day is like the biggest country fair and getting so crowded that many laborers can't get hired, and they beat up or kill one another for a job. But that may last only until the Royal Palm, Flagler's grand hotel in Miami, is completed, and then most of them will go back to where they came from. It is said to be the largest building ever constructed in that town and is situated at the mouth of the Miami River.
 Right now in Linton, we are having a good time because the big sea turtles are still laying their eggs. These are not as big as chicken eggs, but round and with a shell of which I have enclosed a small piece. The turtles lay eggs about one to two feet deep in the sand near the seashore, and in a nest there are approximately two hundred to three hundred eggs. The nests are not so easy to find at first because the turtles disguise their trail from the nest. Still, they leave a trail to the sea about one meter wide. We could have caught turtles of about four hundred and five hundred pounds several times, but I, as well as my neighbor Schroeder, have an aversion to them. Schroeder always collects so many eggs that we can

barely eat them. It's a pity that they will not keep fresh for too long.

Did Fritz get back home safely and what does he say? Did he like it here with me? I now believe that I have a better chance here than if I had stayed in Germany, for I own my land free and clear now and I even have the title to my land. Only, I should have some additional capital to work with, for I want to plant a small pineapple field this year, which will cost me about one hundred dollars. Then I have to have $100 for fertilizer and about $25 for seeds. I have in mind to plant quite a bit of cauliflower this fall. If we should have a light freeze, it wouldn't burn the cauliflower, which fetched a good price throughout the winter. So, if you could let me have another 1,000 marks, I would greatly appreciate it since the sooner the pineapples are planted, the better off I would be. If I postpone the planting until next year, I will be set back again for a year.

Fritz undoubtedly has explained to you how things are around here and what is going on. If you know of anyone who is thinking of emigrating and is inclined to buy land around the Linton area, just send him to me, or tell me about it in advance. For if I could get a number of people here, I would profit considerably, especially if those people could pay for their land in cash. I've learned you have to forge the iron while it's hot.

> Greetings and best wishes to all,
> Yours, Adolf

There was much to explore and discover in those early years. The area was teeming with wildlife and exotic trees that densely populated the landscape. Anna was eager to learn all she could about her new surroundings.

Linton, July 28, 1896

Dear Mother,

    Still I am homesick. I think that it is far worse than the terrible seasickness that plagued me on the long voyage over, and certainly homesickness lasts much longer. This is a lonely land with so few neighbors, and as always, I am still struggling to learn English.
    The Andrews, however, have been the best of friends, and today Annie invited me to join them on an adventure south of here. I bundled Annie inside her basket, taking care to cover it with cheesecloth, which I use for mosquito netting. Once the Andrews brought me across the canal, we stopped at the House of Refuge to prepare for our journey.
    Capt. Andrews showed me how to protect myself from the black funnel clouds of mosquitoes that hover in the marshy areas where we were headed. He said that Ed Hamilton, who had once been a mail carrier who walked barefoot along the beach route, had instructed him how to cake his skin with a weak lye soap made from boiling and leaching alligator fat. Capt. Anderson worked up a thick lather on his arms

and face and let it dry so it would cake on his skin to ward off sand fleas and mosquitoes, or "skeeters," as he calls them. Annie preferred using the Lavender soap sent by Stephen's family in England, so she and I caked our hands and faces with the rich lather. Annie also insisted I wear one of her sun bonnets woven out of dried, sun-bleached palmetto fronds. This I tied on my head with ample cheesecloth.

The three of us headed south over the beach ridge to the sour orange grove just south of Atlantic Avenue. Still visible there on the flat ridge were traces of the old haul-over where Indians dragged their dugouts over the sand using stripped stalks of wild pawpaws as skids. Close to the canal, rich, rank vegetation spread over the mire. It was a fetid marsh of interlocking mangroves where decayed and stinking vegetable matter lodged between the forked roots. Near the bank, gray pelicans roosted on decaying stubs of mangroves. On the larger mangrove trees, flocks of snow-white birds spread their wings on the branches as they draped themselves across the trees.

Threading their way across the soft sand of the beach ridge were vines bearing purple blossoms and velvet seedpods. Verbena and beach lavender grew in and out of the smaller sand dunes. Everywhere, the long-stemmed sea oats with their drooping brown plumes clung to the dunes. Stunted sea grape trees and coco plums grew at random on the sand dunes.

After several miles of walking, we approached the large hammock north of the "Boca Ratones" rocks. Capt. Andrews went ahead alone to make sure that no bears, which frequent the hammocks, were there.

He then led us on to my first view of the towering gumbo limbo trees, whose smooth, tissue-thin bark peels away as it grows. The bark gave off a fragrant odor like spice as we peeled it away. Stephen told us to peel off more bark so he would have it on hand to brew when needed for intestinal upsets. His main purpose in coming here was to stock the House of Refuge for medicinal needs. He planned to gather the resinous gum of the tree for use as an antiseptic to help relieve gout and dysentery for those ill. He also began tapping some of the trees to collect resin to use as glue and varnish. While he was busy doing this, Annie and I began collecting leaves from the gumbo limbo trees, and she explained how to make a tea by steeping the leaves in boiling water. She also went to search for sweet-bay leaves, which she said made a very fragrant beverage like tea.

    We loaded our haversack with the leaves and containers of gum and resin and set our sights on returning home. As I picked up little Annie and slowly turned around, I noticed that a tree with long roots that looked like tentacles had wrapped itself around a cabbage palm. Stephen said it was a strangler fig, a very common tree in our area, and pointed to several others in the hammock. The wild fig grows from a seed dropped by a passing bird and supports itself on a cabbage palm while it slowly sends its tendrils down toward the ground. Once these tendrils reach ground and take root, the fig tree begins to wrap its roots and trunk around the palm, gradually choking it to death as the strangler fig slowly robs the palm of sunlight. So it seems with some of our settlers. Already some have been robbed of hope and strangled by the bleak reality of survival in this wilderness and have left the area to return to their former homes.

    We took the beach route home, cooled by the prevailing southeast trade winds at our back.

Overhead, a flock of screaming gulls sailed past us. Ahead of us, dancing sandpipers left spidery tracks in the wet sand as they darted in and out of the sea foam. The wild beauty of the shore scalloped by wind and waves stretched endlessly before us. The waves flung their crests to the air, sending sprays of salt mist before us. Annie and I paused every now and then to gather colorful shells, which lay scattered among the corks and bits of white coral. Coconuts bobbed about playfully on the ocean tide and washed up on shore amid the litter of driftwood, lumber, and the flotsam of shipwrecks washed up over the years.

At last we reached the House of Refuge, unloaded the haversack, and entertained little Annie with the bright shells and sponges. As Stephen saw me safely back across the canal, I thought of the strangler fig once more and resolved to fight off loneliness and homesickness.

Your loving daughter,
Anna

The Seminole haul-over Anna mentioned in this letter is referred to elsewhere. An 1841-42 military map from the Second Seminole War shows the Linton area. On the map the site is designated "The Orange Grove Haul-Over." Indians hauled their cypress dugouts over the sand ridge near the old sour orange grove. The map also shows a Seminole camp in the vicinity of a large, swampy lake now known as Lake Ida.

Linton, October 1, 1896

Dear Mother,

My heart is heavy with sorrow, Mother, for I have lost a friend. Today was my last chance to visit with Steven and Annie Andrews at the Orange Grove House of Refuge, which the United States government is planning to discontinue and close. How I will miss them since they were my first and dearest friends here. How much they helped both Adolf and me as we struggled to survive here. It was Capt. Andrews who taught me how to cook using palmetto roots as fuel over an open fire. He also showed us how to make thatched roofs out of cabbage palm fronds for our barn and shed and how to fish for tarpon and red snapper.

Annie met me at the lighter, and after we made our way out of the mangroves and muck, together we edged carefully across the wide swampland that stretches from the canal to the sloping sand ridge. The morass was rank and teeming with fiddler crabs and blue land crabs whose claws threatened us menacingly as we crossed.

Once across the morass, we sat on the crest of the wide dune ridge, embraced by sea oats blown by the wind. It is our favorite spot to overlook both land and sea. For it is here on the western side of the ridge that a narrow stream of water flows freely before it fans out again into a broad, boggy area stretching north and south. The stream lies between the high ridge of sand and the muck land. It meanders slowly at random, at times a shallow trickle clogged with sawgrass, at times a flowing silent stream, only to spread out again in sawgrass. Some months ago, Annie told me the stream is actually a creek beginning near the south end of Lake Worth that flows south until it fans out and settles in sawgrass a little north of the House of Refuge. Some locals have come to call it "Steve's Creek" after Capt. Andrews.

Mrs. Andrews held little Annie, now twelve and a half months old, as we talked about our times together. How sad to think that she is leaving here after all we've shared together. Now she will be the traveler and the stranger instead of me. Even in our sadness, we could not help but smile at little Annie struggling to stand in the shifting sand.

In my melancholy, I looked at the stream for a long time and slowly felt strengthened. How much it reminded me of the verse in Psalm 46, "There is a river, the streams of which shall make glad the City of God." Even though the House of Refuge will be closed and the sign above the door bearing the name of Zion has already been removed, I will always think of Zion as my spiritual refuge in this wilderness. Yet my heart is heavy with sorrow, Mother, for I have lost a friend.

My love to you and the family,
Anna

Located in an isolated, windswept area, the Orange Grove House of Refuge was surrounded on three sides by saw palmettos. It was officially closed in October 1896. (Courtesy of Delray Beach Historical Society)

As the first few years of hardship passed, Adolf grew hopeful that he would eventually succeed as a farmer in Linton.

Linton, April 21, 1897

My Father,

    I cannot write anything good about this year's weather. We have had many problems with the storms and heavy rains. Our typical rainy season in October and November was unusually bad this year, and therefore our crop season was swept away and we made a poor showing. We are hoping still that everything from now on will go well and that things will get better.

    In spite of the setbacks, I am still making out well in my daily work. On tomatoes I make my biggest profits, and they are bringing much higher prices this year. I have up to now shipped forty-six crates of tomatoes, and the weight of each crate was approximately fifty pounds. For each one I get two dollars in profit. I can't believe that I am doing so well and am making so much. I am now doing well enough to pay all my bills. It is a very pleasing picture. So with all the expenses for my farm taken care of, my living costs are small except for the absolute essentials we must buy.

    My pineapples have grown well this year, and I have extended them a whole acre. They can grow now until the next winter, and we don't have to do anything to care for them until winter comes around again. There is nothing to be done with them except a little kindness and attention from time to time. I hope we can even make a small profit from them. We always hope for the best, and later on, if nothing comes in, what can one do?

Also, with my chickens everything goes well. They are worth the while and all the trouble they take. I take great pleasure and comfort to know they are doing so well. I have now forty chickens. Luckily, I'm selling about one dozen eggs each and every day, which comes to twenty-five or thirty cents. Up to this time, I've had three chickens sitting, and already I have seventeen eggs waiting to hatch.

Perhaps our inheritance from the Schwarz estate will show up some day. Absolutely nothing has been heard from anyone regarding this matter. I can't imagine what is taking so long. The German Consul in Illinois is helping us with the legalities. Yet the Consul is made up mostly of lawyers, and they know better than anyone else how to take the money out of someone's pocket. I think it more likely that the German breweries will go out of business before the authorities turn over our inheritance money! And you know what an absurd improbability that is.

I haven't been able to get far away from my place this year, and I cannot take any time off from all the work required on my property.

Greetings and best wishes,
Yours, Adolf

Hofman's Early Real Estate Ventures

As keen as Adolf's interest was in acquiring farmland, his ambitions were not limited merely to farming. At times, Hofman took another view of land use. On several occasions he purchased property solely for real estate purposes. Sources show that he negotiated to purchase the house and acreage of Peter Luhrs located near Palm Trail, north of Northeast Eighth Street, when Luhrs left Linton in 1896. Adolf rented the Luhrs house to several different people during the next few years. He finally received the deed to the land on June 18, 1900. In 1901 he rented the house to Sophie Frey, who had just arrived in town, for $3.50 a month and eventually sold her the land in 1903.

Adolf made another early venture into real estate. On June 16, 1897, he bought a house close to the railroad station for an absurdly low price in hopes of renting it to visitors during the winter. The Florida East Coast railway brought scores of visitors seeking adventure and possible settlement. Adolf realized this real estate potential and began investing in more property for rental or resale purposes. He also secured property in the heart of town. He purchased Lots 1, 2, and 3 of Block 100 on Atlantic Avenue from L.G. Lyman and Kate M. Lyman on January 26, 1907. This was prime property on the main street in downtown Delray.

*Adolf's early letters narrate some of the
exciting adventures and opportunities
he had during his first years in Linton.*

Linton, June 16, 1897

Dear Father,

The fat times have begun here again since our lives on turtle eggs and turtle meat have resumed. Just yesterday at twelve midnight, I killed a turtle of about six hundred pounds. If only one could better preserve the meat—it is spoiled in four to five days even when heavily salted. So only the best parts get eaten; the rest is fed to the chickens. And then the hunt is on once more, for if you are with three or four men, you can be sure to get one every time. The chickens get plenty of these turtle scraps to eat as well as gator meat. My neighbor Schroeder and I just recently shot two alligators, which I also fed to my chickens.

Since I bought a house today with pineapples and furnishings quite close to the railroad station for $100, I want to ask you to send me another $50 to $100. I wouldn't have taken this house if it had not been for this ridiculously low price and the fact that the pineapples are of the best variety. Their planting last year alone cost $100. And then I have the house of which just the lumber costs $115. The property also has on it a boat worth $20, bananas, mangoes, oranges, and other trees besides. This man wants to leave because his wife doesn't want to stay here under any circumstances. She is a grand American lady, and life here is too boring for her, for there is no concert or theater as there is in the North. And among the Anglo-Americans the men have to do as the women wish.

The Model Land Company tried to charge three hundred dollars for the property. Some others wanted to buy this house but had not yet paid for their land. Moreover, they did not own any property in the town. Everyone who buys land from the company gets property for building for free. Since I have already paid for my land, my property allotted for building has already been registered since last year. I asked the company if I could exchange the property with the one that has the house and pineapples, and they agreed without any problems. It only cost me a three-dollar transfer fee. During the winter I can always rent that house and collect five to six dollars rent per month.

I would have gotten along with my money except for my wanting to plant more pineapples, and the more I plant the better I get ahead. For the growing of vegetables here is pure lottery—play—one year you can make an immense profit and another year you can lose as much. Therefore I'd like to ask you to send me the money as quickly as possible since I want to plant my pineapples already in July.

With best greetings,
Yours, Adolf

Linton, June 18, 1897

Dear Mother,

This afternoon is set aside for baking since I must use the turtle eggs before they spoil. Some people claim they can be saved up to a week. Who would ever imagine using the eggs of turtles for cooking? Of course, we must use more of them in place of hen's eggs since turtle eggs are smaller. Adolf scooped up a bucketful of eggs on the beach last night where he joined other men all bent on snatching the small eggs before the bears or raccoons devoured them.

Adolf told me how the large loggerhead turtles swim in to shore at the same season every year to deposit their eggs at night. They slowly drag their way up to drier, higher sand to a point beyond the high tide line. There they furiously dig large holes some eighteen inches deep with their flapping arms, or fore flippers, scattering the sand haphazardly into high piles.

Once the scores of eggs have been deposited, they carefully cover these holes again and pack down and flatten the sand by dropping the underside of their bodies on the mound over and over again. To deceive their enemies, they even smooth the nest over and make false tracks in the sand to disguise the real location of the nest. Then they lumber back down to the ocean, dragging their heavy bodies into the surf, where they swim away in the darkness.

The men are quick to dig up and seize the eggs because they know full well that animals will plunder the nests in no time. And if they don't get them, the sea gulls are sure to gulp down the soft, helpless newborns when they hatch and scurry to the sea. So around this time each year, the men make nighttime excursions to the beach, and each man brings home as many eggs as can be used before they spoil. Keeping food from spoiling is forever our problem here in Linton. But the turtles and their eggs are always plentiful at this time of year.

I plan to use my eggs in baking breads and cakes today. Flour and other staples are brought from Lantana by the Lymans on their boat twice a week, and I am well supplied in that regard. Perhaps I will also make rabbit stew as we did at home since Adolf has bagged and skinned several rabbits with his .22 rifle. He carries the rifle with him quite often, for one never knows when quail will alight in the area, and they prove such a treat for us. Often he must shoot squirrels out of the fruit trees because they are forever scavenging the trees and damaging each fruit by nibbling small chunks of fruit before scampering to another tree.

We planted some of the fruit trees only two years ago, and, even though the trees are still small, already they bear full-sized fruit. Adolf has taken to grafting trees. In Florida the cleft grafting goes marvelously well as a result of the warm temperature and heavy rain. He cuts a good-sized slit into the stock tree and inserts a wedge-shaped graft from another fruit tree, then carefully binds the two together with cloth and cord. The grafted shoot grows quickly, and a better-tasting fruit buds and matures.

His greatest success is grafting mango trees, a tropical fruit some say is from Malaysia, some say from India. It is a large oval fruit that turns a glorious *golden red as it ripens in early June. The peel is thick and oily and is usually peeled away before eating, while the pulp is juicy and both sweet and tart at the same time. It is unlike any taste I can describe to you. Adolf always plants the large mango seeds in tin cans filled with soil, and the process yields more thriving plants. Thus his crop grows steadily. He also grows palm trees merely by splitting coconuts open and placing them in soil, which here is primarily made up of sand from the former beaches of ancient shorelines. Coconut palms are sprouting everywhere in Linton now that the locals know how easy they are to plant.*

I must hasten to my baking while the turtle eggs are fresh. Perhaps we will also cook some of them for breakfast tomorrow. They taste every bit as good as any other egg, though these reptile eggs with their tough leathery skins are harder to crack. I think that instead of the rabbit stew, I will use the turtle meat Adolf brought home the other night. He was careful to cut it cross-grain as close as possible in order to make it tender just as Capt. Andrews showed the men. I'll batter it and fry it for supper tonight.

> *My greetings and love to everyone,*
> *Anna*

To draw tourists and promote settlement in South Florida, the Florida East Coast Railway published colorful information booklets with timetables and hotel fares. This booklet describes Linton as having "as good water as can be found on the coast." The rates for The Chapman House are listed as "$2.00 per day with special rates for the week or season. Half mile to ocean beach; rock road direct to bath house. Fine bathing."

Linton, October 10, 1897

Dear Father,

It has been a long time since I've heard from you, and I am eager to hear the news from home. I trust that you are in good health and that all goes well with the family.

The Florida East Coast Railway continues to bring more and more people to town. The train now travels back and forth daily carrying visitors and settlers. Adventure seekers come to hunt or fish, and families come to settle in increasing numbers. The FEC company boasts about Linton's pure drinking water and its nearness to the ocean.

The economy in the States is at this time miserable. It seems I am always hard at work and I am always putting money out on top here with expectation that I might not get it back anyway. In Linton the economy is as weak as it was two years ago when I first came here. It could even be that in four years it will be as bad as it is today. Yet I hope that another time will bring us more prosperity for all of our hard work.

We have had unbelievably good weather here in Linton. Soon I will be planting. Once again, I plan to have as my crops potatoes, beans, cabbages, and eggplant. I will also plant collards and turnips. This winter, I am hoping to have tomatoes planted as my main cash crop for market. In this way, I will be like any other American farmer by having a main crop to harvest for sale. Along with the other farmers in Linton, I ship my produce regularly by means of the railway, which runs through the heart of Linton.

Be sure to ask Fritz if he still has the shark teeth and also the alligator teeth he took back. And does he still have the hide from the alligator we shot and skinned when he visited me last year. I am also curious to know if he has the turtle shell he took back with him.

With me it goes well and my health is ever good. In all respects I am fine.

Best greetings to you,
Always, Adolf

In a letter written to Adolf in 1897, Fritz answered some of Adolf's questions. Fritz wrote, "The teeth that I took from a shark and from some alligators were mounted and fashioned into a brooch for my bride. This brooch is admired by everyone." Such souvenir jewelry made from the teeth of exotic animals was popular in this era.

Although the residents of Linton went about their daily lives somewhat removed from outside concerns, the town was sometimes touched by the larger sphere of world events.

Linton, August 10, 1898

Dear Father,

At last I get the chance to write again. I have much news to report. No doubt you have read the war stories in your newspapers. Our news here about the Spanish-American War is that the peace may be near since they are working on a treaty. I am eager to know the results of the peace negotiations. It is certain that the United States will take Puerto Rico. How it will be with Cuba and the Philippine Islands, we do not know yet.

Some Americans have become so carried away with the war that they think they could conquer the whole world. However, any other major power could have had the same success over such a down-and-out force like Spain.

In Florida there is much flurry and activity about the war. The military is in large numbers in Tampa, Miami, and Key West. Tampa is all but taken over by the military. Day after day, I watch trainload after trainload of soldiers pass through Linton night and day carrying soldiers on their way to Miami. I even hear the trains at night roll by loaded with battalions of soldiers. But, now, they are starting to send some of the military back.

As a result of the annexation of Hawaii and maybe now also Puerto Rico and Cuba, the German sugar industry will suffer greatly. In Hawaii, supposedly they grow sugar cane with the richest sugar content. Various American businesses have moved to Hawaii and in short time have cornered the sugar market. The sugar industry has grown big in the United States, and the Americans will satisfy their needs themselves and will no longer be dependent on Germany for sugar.

The farmers here in Linton have it much better this year. The pineapple harvest is here now and is very good. We had a great drought during most of the summer, but now we are getting hit with considerably many showers and heavy rains. Although they are beautiful, the thunderstorms bring large masses of mosquitoes to pester us during our harvest work. The mosquitoes are so bad that it is impossible to work in early morning or evening, so heavy is the infestation. They come in such heavy droves that you can put your hand right through a wall of mosquitoes and leave a hole there.

It is a good year, and all is going well. I am always feeling good here, and thanks to God, I am always in a good state of health. In fact, I have never been sick a day here in Linton, and that is amazing when you consider all we have to endure. You have to put up with many obstacles and persist with a lot of hard work in order to endure here. The summer heat is unbearable, but if you can get farther into the year, then it is indeed very beautiful. The same is true with my struggles.

Once I got through with clearing my land and conquering the big obstacles, I felt I had made some *progress*, and things began to look better. Alligators and rattlesnakes are still seen often, but if one crosses my path, I am quick to shoot it. There are so many beautiful things growing wild here that I never had time to notice until now.

I read in the paper that there are considerably many Social Democrats in the Reichstag, and it looks like the Social Democrats might take over Germany. And much is being written over here about Bismarck's death. I close in the hope that I will hear something from you.

Yours,
Adolf

Anna faithfully continued to use her German Lutheran hymnal and prayer book during her years in Linton. (Photo by Michael Hopkins, CPP)

Despite the rigors of frontier life and the separation from their fatherland, Adolf and Anna continued to practice their Christian faith by worshiping in the tradition of the German Evangelical Lutheran Church.

Linton, October 5, 1898

Dear Mother,

I have everything ready for the arrival of the Reverend Edward Fischer. Our family Bible is placed in the sitting room along with my prayer book and my *Christliches Vergissmeinnicht*, [a type of diary and daily devotions book] which I use to write down events as they happen in Linton. Pastor Fischer is the Lutheran minister who comes to call on us twice a year as he travels up and down the east coast of Florida as a circuit rider. Adolf met him earlier this year at the railway station, where Pastor Fischer was inquiring the possible whereabouts of fellow Lutherans in hopes of founding a church in Linton.

Adolf asked him to conduct worship services and administer Holy Communion at our house, and thus the first Lutheran worship service was held in our home. And we are not alone. Frank Haller, though a Roman Catholic, and Otto Schroeder join us in these worship services along with several others. How good it is to hear the gospel preached in German again and to receive the Holy Sacrament. Much more wonderful it would be to have a Lutheran church of our own in

Linton, but for now, I must be content that church services are conducted in our home. Pastor Fischer has given Adolf a Concordia sermon book along with a liturgy book and other prayer books to use when the pastor is making his circuit calls. Adolf continues Bible readings and devotional services at our house every Sunday for our family and friends. In this way we keep our faith in some troubled times here in Linton.

Already it has been three years since Adolf and I came to this frontier, and on this same day three years ago, Adolf first set foot in Linton. During these years God has blessed us with good health and bountiful land. Adolf's restless energy is devoted to expanding his land, and he seldom tires of grafting new trees or extending his pineapple fields. His wanderlust for far off places has settled firmly in Linton.

No one could ask for a more hostile, untamed frontier as the one we faced. At first, even the underbrush and trees were untamed enemies. The cabbage palms rustled and made a crackling sound in the hot winds, and their harsh scratching scolded us for coming. The raucous birds consumed the Florida holly bushes for their greedy feasts. Everything was alien and at first forbidding.

Now, after three hard years, we have the house and the barn, and soon Adolf will begin building his packing shed north of the pump area. God has bestowed His goodness on us, and under His providential care we have survived and endured in Linton. We expect Pastor Fischer to arrive shortly, and we will worship with him.

     Your loving daughter,
     Anna

The only certainties for the early settlers of Linton were constant change and the persistent threat of failure.

Linton, November 20, 1898

Dear Mother,

Make certain to take note of my new return address, for recently the most unusual thing has happened. Six leaders in our little community met in the schoolhouse in the heart of town and voted to change the name of our town from Linton to Delray.

Many of our townspeople have become exceedingly disheartened by the bad times that have befallen the village of Linton. Two bad freezes within the last two years ruined the crops and drove some settlers out of town. What is worse is that Mr. Linton himself left the area last year and has not returned. Mr. Linton encouraged people to settle here by selling five-acre tracts of land in town. Adolf paid in full for one of those tracts.

Now Mr. Linton is gone, and he has failed to make payments on his own mortgage notes. So Linton's creditors have threatened to foreclose on his holdings, and who knows what has become of the money Adolf paid Mr. Linton? Time and time again, people came to associate the name of Linton with failure and were clamoring to change the name of the town in hopes of seeing better times.

Added to this is the confusion arising from the name of a town called Linden near the west coast of Florida. At times, our mail was sent to Linden, and their mail was sent to us since the two names were so similar. It created considerable confusion and delayed correspondence for all of us.

So the six leaders met last night in the schoolhouse to select a new name for our town. A sizeable group of our townspeople are from Michigan. In fact, three of the leaders are from Detroit and suggested the name of a Detroit suburb named Delray, where Mr. Blackmer comes from. Because Mr. Linton has vanished, they chose Mr. Blackmer as our new leader and renamed our town Delray.

I am told the word "Delray" was originally spelled "del Rey," or "Del Rey," the name of a town in Mexico. The words in Spanish mean "of the king." What a royal title for our little town! Yet another word in another language for me to remember. Who could imagine such a mixture of languages and cultures in a village so small as ours?

When I heard that the word was Spanish and meant "of the king," I remembered the wild sour orange grove and the ruins of the rock wall that Capt. Andrews said might have been the remains of a Spanish settlement. No doubt their land grant to explore and settle here was from their king, and the land was rightfully his. It seems an odd twist of fate that our leaders happened upon this word unknowingly and for another reason. And so it seems to me that the old Spanish settlers have returned to rule again, if only in name, under the claim of their king.

How legends grow! For in the three years we have lived here, already the small stream between the muck land and the beach ridge, known as Steve's

Creek, has grown into legend and has become the "Spanish River" in the minds of some newcomers who believe the tall tales that at one time a river flowed through this area.

Remember, Mama, to address your letters from now on to "Anna Hofmann, Delray, Florida, Nord-Amerika." There is always constant change and activity here. Perhaps we shall prosper under the new name.

Love from your daughter,
Anna

Records in the National Archives indicate that the United States Post Office officially changed the name of the town from Linton to Delray on November 19, 1898. The name was officially changed once again to Delray Beach on January 1, 1928.

Delray, June 29, 1899

Dear Father,

 I received your letter and I would like to follow your wish to come to my sister Emma's wedding if only it would be possible for me. But it is not possible because the month of February is the most unsuitable month for me. That is the time I have to work the most; moreover, I could not leave my farm anyway since I have no one else to manage it for me.
 I would have loved to send you a box with pineapples and bananas, if only that would not cost too much duty for customs, and then again, I am not sure whether it would arrive in good condition.
 In the northern states they have a very rough winter this year. Here we barely feel any of it. But we do have the north wind, and shortly after Christmas, we had a little night frost, which did not cause that much damage. So far in 1899, we have had rather warm weather, and that is good for all the crops.
 After three and a half years in the wilderness here, I would have loved to come together with my brothers and sisters, but I am really not able to come. I wish Emma all the happiness for her marriage and new life.

    With the best wishes to you,
      Yours, Adolf
P.s. The name Linton has been changed and is now Delray; therefore, this is my new address:
     A. Hofmann
     Delray, Florida
     U. St. Amerika

The Hofman home stood alone, a half mile north of Linton's city limits. The house faced east, overlooking the canal, and had no road or driveway in front of the house. It was surrounded by sandspurs, white sugar sand, and wild morning glories.
Left to right: William, Annie, and Clara in 1908

In the early days, West Palm Beach was the only semblance of a large town near Linton. It had mushroomed from a boisterous tent city, which housed the construction workers who built Flagler's Royal Poinciana Hotel, into a sizeable city. By 1899 Clematis Street was the main shopping street and a mecca for Linton residents who traveled the distance for its shops and services.

Linton-Delray, September 20, 1899

Dear Mother,

    Along with this letter, you should receive a photograph of Annie and me. I took her with me to West Palm Beach to have our portrait taken several weeks before her fourth birthday. What a time of it we had on our long journey.
    Since the morning train through Linton travels south, we were left to take the horse and wagon service provided by John Eggers. We joined several others, including Mrs. Tasker and Otto Schroeder, boarded the wagon seats, and headed west toward the county rock road for the long ride north. The narrow road seemed treacherous at first, and I held Annie close on the wide plank. As the horse steadied himself and lumbered along, the methodical clopping of his hooves lulled Annie to sleep.
    When we arrived in West Palm Beach, I located the photography studio of Mr. O'Donoghue, who by prior arrangement was expecting us. Annie was

Anna and four-year-old Annie made the seventeen-mile trip to West Palm Beach to have their photograph taken at the O'Donoghue Studio in 1899.

keenly alert and quite intrigued by the camera. I have selected a pose for you, Mama, to place in the family album at Erpfingen. If only the photograph could have captured Annie's pale blue-gray eyes. Surely she has Adolf's eye color and boundless energy. For she was so playful that it took Mr. O'Donoghue, his assistant, and myself considerable effort to get her to sit still long enough to capture the pose.

From the photography studio we walked several blocks down Clematis Street in each direction, looking for dry goods stores where I could purchase yard goods, ribbons, and other notions not available in Linton. I was told that the Mercantile Bazaar was the best place in town for notions and yard goods.

At last came the long ride home in the wagon with the others. We had traveled some miles when suddenly, Otto Schroeder jumped up and yelled, "Over there, look, a wildcat!" Sure enough, a wildcat was following the wagon, evidently enticed by the smell of smoked pork and cured hams bound for Linton. He was so close that his fierce eyes, mirrored in the wagon lantern, glinted yellow, and he crouched low, looking ready to pounce on the back of the wagon. Old John Eggers wheeled around, raised his shotgun, and blasted the creature point blank. The stunned wildcat sank, its blood streaming into the sand, and we left behind us the lifeless body on the cold stone road. With death behind us, we sat silent as the wheels wore on.

Isolated pines dotted the horizon and darkened in the dusk. Cabbage palms and palmettos skirted every bend in the road. Somehow the scratching of their leaves comforted me as we headed home. I welcomed the whisper of the wheels in the soft sand.

The clattering of the palmettos seemed like conversation to me. I once hated, but now respect, the tough roots they sink deep into the ground, determined to survive. For so it is with us in Linton, as I still call Delray. As tangled and matted as this landscape seems, we wield our power over it. Some things endure and bid us home—stars, moon, sea, and sky. As we labor in the land, we reenact the eternal cycle of planting and reaping.

In the deepening dusk settling over the wilderness, all things headed for home. Gopher turtles dragged their heavy shells over the sand, flattening weeds and sandspurs. Far away, from some distant waterway, a lone blue heron rose, soared slowly over the horizon, and headed for home in the west. As the sky dimmed, the ancient wrestling of the earth with its endless struggle between life and death subsided for the night.

You must share the photograph with all the family, Mama, and keep us close to you in that way. Look at us often, Mama, and remember us here across the sea, for a photo album is as close as I'll ever come to my childhood home again.

Far off, a few lamps in Linton sputter in the gathering dusk. I know I am truly home here in Linton, home with Adolf and Annie, at home with this wild earth and its untamed land in this far-flung frontier. All around me, stars, moon, sea, and sky. Before me, Linton and home.

Your loving daughter,
Anna

Pineapples were the mainstay of many Delray farmers, including Adolf. The "pines" were planted in patches or in vast fields called plantations. Packing houses were sometimes called "pineries." As Adolf's pineapple patches expanded to cover more and more acreage, Hofman called his fields a plantation. Even though pineapples were his most productive crop, Adolf could not benefit financially because of the tight control the Florida East Coast Railway had on market prices. He soon became disillusioned with the railway for its unfair freight charges that discriminated against Delray growers and other South Florida farmers.

Delray, January 13, 1901

Dear Father,

I have received your letter, but I am not always quick to reply. I can't think of much to write about at this time of year. This winter we have truly had cold weather, perhaps the coldest as far back as I can remember from my years of being here. In fact, the weather has not been good for most of the winter.

How I wait in hopes that warmer weather will come our way yet this winter, for I am looking to plant beans as soon as the weather permits. Some frost has come our way, and we have never had this long a frost, and what is worse, it is staying on the ground. With my pineapples everything is about the same, and I expect a good crop when the time comes. I have extended my fields to produce an even greater crop this year.

Of course, with the pineapple market we always have to worry about the competition from Cuba. And to compete in the pineapple market, we Floridians have to pay high charges to the railroad for our freight. We have heard that the railroad even refuses to load pineapples south of Miami since Cuba supplies far cheaper pineapples. In America we send over corn and meat to their farmers to benefit them, and yet we farmers here get nothing in return. The Florida East Coast Railway controls everything to its advantage, and we in Delray are forced to pay high freight.

Perhaps our inheritance from the Schwarz estate will come forth one day. But about that matter I have heard nothing. Fritz wrote that the matter lingers in the courts, and we have nothing to do but to wait and remain patient. Fritz should once again write a letter to the German Consulate to let them know that we have not forgotten the matter.

> My best greetings,
> Yours, Adolf

Delray, November 11, 1901

Dear Grandma Dreher,

How are you across the sea? I wish I could visit you. Today Mama and I worked in the attic. Mama put fresh coconut in the mousetraps. It works. Like cheese.

A funny thing happened the other day. Papa tied up his horse and wagon at the railroad station and went inside. Lightning struck close by and our horse pulled loose and ran all the way to Boynton. With the wagon.

We think it is funny, but Papa doesn't think so. Please write me soon.

Your loving granddaughter,
Annie

Delray, April 27, 1902

Dear Father,

Your letter arrived some weeks ago. I wanted to write sooner, but I put it off from one week to the next because presently I have so much to do that I can only take care of the most urgent correspondence. We have now very warm weather, exceedingly dry, but the vegetables and fruit are nevertheless in excellent shape. However, the worms in the vegetables are very bad, so that one half has to be thrown away. We are busily shipping produce, but prices leave a lot to be desired. Because of the strong increase of settlers during the last few years, so much is being planted that prices have dropped a lot, and only those who operate on a large scale make good money.

Just now a new company has been organized. They plan to build a navigable canal through the Everglades, a big swamp west of here that extends thirty to forty miles to the south. Thereby in doing so, they want to drain several million acres for planting sugar cane and vegetables. According to experiments, sugar cane is expected to do excellent there, also rice and cassava, a starch plant that has high starch content. There are already several starch factories where the starch is extracted.

You wrote whether I am still not in a position to get married, but here I have been married for five and a half years. I wrote you about it, but you gave me no answer to this; therefore, I did not mention it again in later letters. I have two children, both are girls, one five years, the other four months old. I wrote you earlier this year that my second daughter, named Clara, was born at home on January 7 of this year. We were fortunate to have the local midwife help with the delivery. Both girls are flourishing; they are strong and healthy children. My wife is also in excellent health.

I think you are far from having cause for complaint about the cost of your laborers. Here they pay for good farmhands $1.25 up to $2.00, hence in German money, 5 to 8 marks per day. I only hire one man when it is extremely urgent. At other times, my wife must help me vigorously, which she does willingly with no complaints. In this respect I am a fortunate man.

> Greetings to all,
> Yours, Adolf and wife
> and children,
> Annie, Clara

SOPHIE FREY ∞ PIONEER SETTLER

The Florida frontier drew stalwart settlers. One of the strongest women ever to endure those pioneer days was Sophie Frey, who came to Delray in September of 1901 with five children in hand. Sophie Frey was an industrious German who became known for her tenacious and untiring work. As the next letter reveals, she lived in a small house north of the Hofmans down by the canal. She and her children became good friends with the Hofman family. In addition to rearing her children and maintaining her farm, Sophie wrote down her life story in a journal, or autobiography, titled "Life's Bitter Sweet." Her granddaughter, Dorothy Zill Susleck, a Delray Beach native, shared Sophie's journal with me and donated it to the Delray Beach Historical Society's Cornell Archives Room. Anna's letters of May 3, 1902 and December 26, 1928 incorporate Sophie's narration of her pioneer days quoted word for word from her autobiography.

Delray, May 3, 1902

Dear Mother,

This morning I heard a knock on the front door, and I was pleased to see Sophie Frey and her daughter Carrie through the glass panels. I hardly ever get to see them even though they are our neighbors across the fields. Since Clara is still a baby and Sophie has her children and farm work, there is never time to visit.

Sophie came to America from Speyer, Germany years ago. She was living on the lower east side of New York City, where she was doing fancy needlework to help support her family. Later, she went to New Jersey, continued her needlework, which was so good that it was much in demand, and managed to save some money. She heard of land available in Linton and somehow got in touch with Adolf for more information. What I remember most is that she arrived in September of 1901 with only $40.00 in cash and five children.

While Annie took Carrie outside to explore, I asked Sophie to sit and talk a while. I especially wanted to hear the details of how she came to Delray and why she settled here. She told me the whole story in her own words.

"For years my husband was a heavy drinker. Whenever he had too much to drink, he lost control of himself and would become hateful and abusive to me. After years of putting up with him, I made plans to leave him and escape to a new place, far away.

"My first step was to write to the Postmaster of Linton, asking him if he could let me know if there was a house to rent somewhere in town. I wrote in German, and he gave my letter to a German who had lots of land. This turned out to be your husband. Adolf offered me the little three-room house he owned north of you, down by the canal, and five acres of land for $3.50 a month. I wrote that I would take it.

"My second step was to write to the Clyde Steamship Line for fare on a ship from New York to Jacksonville and ask if they would give me a reduction as a settler in Florida. They wrote back they would give me two cabins and good meals for steerage passage. My third step was to write to the Florida

East Coast Railway at St. Augustine for reductions as settlers, and the answer came right back that my reduced ticket would lay ready at Jacksonville."

I asked her, "How did you manage to get here with your belongings and five children?"

"We packed two trunks, one bureau, my sewing machine, and some eatables for the first part of the journey. We arrived in Florida on September 8, and it was 9:30 in the morning when we reached Linton by train. Adolf received word and sent a horse and wagon to the depot. All the kids climbed on board the wagon, and we went through wooded land a mile and a quarter out of town, and with every word we spoke, we swallowed a dozen mosquitoes.

"At last we were at the house and ready to rest, but there were no screens in the windows. Sand flies, mosquitoes, and roaches were something new to us. All the children were crying, but I told them they might just as well stop since there was no one to listen to them, and we were here to stay with plenty of work ahead of us in the days to come. That night, we lay on the floor on everything we brought with us. The next day, we cleaned the house and cooked on a campfire. There was nothing in the house."

I told Sophie that before Adolf bought the place, it was the old Luhrs house built in 1895. I continued, "It may be a small house, but it's a good, sturdy one."

Sophie continued, "The next day, we fought off the mosquitoes and went to work. We found old boards and made beds out of them. Then we found a chicken house, got six chickens for $3.00, and started to plant the garden. All the money we had when we came to Florida was $40.00, and I was too proud to ask for help.

"Every morning at 6:00 a.m. I went to the fields, had dinner at noon, and worked in the fields again until dark, but I was never tired. I did all the sewing and washing after dark and got along fine. There were five acres of land with the house, and my first crop of lima beans, tomatoes, string beans, peppers, and cabbages was shipped north on the railroad. I made $400.

"Later, I asked your husband if he would sell me the rest of the land, seventeen and a half acres, or all of the plat from the Florida East Coast Railway to the East Coast Canal, five hundred feet both ways. He agreed to do it for me. I paid $22 on the land and the rest I could pay whenever I had the money. The oldest girl went to the fields with me, and the second went to school. The eight-year-old boy also went to school. The six-year-old boy and the baby played in the field while I worked."

"I know how that is, with Annie and Clara beside me in the fields."

"I continued to clear more of my land to have it ready for the next planting season. There was ragweed as high as six or seven feet, which I cut down. I cleared two acres of farmland with my own hands, made ditches, made my rows for the beans and tomatoes, put all the fertilizer in, and the seed, and when the crop was ready to harvest, sent it to market."

"You've worked harder and longer than most men. You seem driven to work and prosper for the sake of your children."

"Work is my only hope, and the children give me strength."

The girls returned, and it was time to say goodbye. I stood at the front door and watched Sophie leave, walking straight and strong with a fierce pride and independence. Few can prevail with such courage. So it goes. It is our lot to work all our days. We go from strength to strength nurturing the soil, which, in turn, nurtures us and sustains us in earth's age-old pattern of tilling and reaping. So are we all toilers of the soil, keepers of the earth.

>Your loving daughter,
>Anna

Sophie Frey, a 1901 pioneer settler, stands in front of her home, which was the first house built in Linton in 1895. Left to right: Sophie Frey, Clara Hofman, Annie Hofman, Margarete Frey, about 1917

Delray, Florida, Dec. 25, 1902

Dear Father,

I got your letter today and will reply immediately. In answer to your question that you've asked before, I have now already been married for six years. My wife comes from the Schwäbische Alb and came to Florida together with relatives of hers. She comes from a good Christian family. She had small finances and little property. Only her mother survives; her father died before she arrived here. He had suffered a long illness, which was also very costly, and his sons were not yet old enough to take care of the small farm, which consequently took a bad turn and was rather run down. But now their circumstances have improved again.

I am completely satisfied with my choice, for she can very well understand my situation and all my moods. She is a very hard worker—and that is of the greatest value here—and is always content even though we have gone through some very hard times. Of course it wouldn't have hurt to have found a wealthier bride, but I think one of those would have run away long since, and wealth doesn't always bring happiness.

My two girls are strong, healthy children. I send a photograph of them, but that was already taken in July. My youngest has grown considerably since then and will be one year old on January 7 and has never been ill for an hour. A doctor has yet to see the inside of my house, and I thank God for keeping my family always in such good health.

Clara and Annie posed for this formal picture taken 1902, which Adolf mentions in the letter he wrote on December 25, 1902.

So much for my family—if you want to know more, then ask specific questions. My older girl always wants to know so much about Germany and enjoys it royally when my wife's family sends her a small gift once in a while.

The year 1902 generally was a good one here. The year 1901 for me was a total loss and I lost a lot of money. I could not make up my expenses. Actually, I ship green beans, and my wife and I have to pick beans every day up to our heads to get finished. The beans bring a good price now, and if the frost stays away, I can make good money.

Up north they are supposed to have very cold weather. I also read that you have very cold weather in Germany. I wish you could once come to us during the winter. It is wonderful here, and I also have something good to drink now. I make wine from pineapples and also from bananas, and it's no second to the best Rhine wine.

> Yours, Adolf with wife
> and children,
> Annie and Clara

Delray, February 23, 1903

Dear Father,

I received the money you sent, and I am extending my best thanks for that. We are truly hard at work this winter. It is the warmest winter since I have been here.

This year the land here is worth more and would draw a very good price if I so wanted to sell. It is possible I could really benefit from selling land if I so desired, but I think it is better not to, for what else could I do in this area but farm, and where would I go without my land?

Other farmers left to try their hand at different things. I recall that many families left Linton at the beginning of the Spanish-American War and went to Miami to try their luck. But almost all of them returned. A yellow fever epidemic sent them back to Delray. That brings back other memories from the past. While we lived in tents at first, Mr. Linton helped the engineer lay out and name the streets. They set cabbage palms up and down the length of Atlantic Avenue. He also had four cabbage palms planted at each street intersection. The men were eager to build houses as soon as possible, and some even took driftwood and lumber that washed on shore from shipwrecks.

Delray continues to change. Now much building is going on in town. I am having a large addition, which will give us more room, built on to the back of our house.

We greet you with kind regards,
Adolf and wife and children

Life at Home

Adolf and Anna continued to live in their house built in 1896. The original two-story structure faced east to catch the coastal breezes. There were no roads or streets to interrupt their sweeping view of the canal. Cabbage palms, palmettos, and scrub oak led down to the mangroves on the bank of the canal.

Two additions were added to the house years later, one in 1903, and one in 1925. With these two additions the house became a rambling frame and stucco structure. It reflected several of the architectural styles that evolved in Delray as the town grew. In the 1925 addition, the front entrance was relocated to face what is now Northeast Seventh Avenue. However, for decades Northeast Seventh Avenue was not graded or paved beyond Northeast Fifth Street. It remained a private entrance lane to the Hofman property. In deference to Adolf's status as a pioneer settler, the city did not extend the avenue through his property until after his death in 1953. Likewise, Northeast Sixth Street was never completed as a through street between Northeast Seventh and Northeast Eighth Avenues because Adolf's mango groves and packing house were located on that spot for over five decades.

The Hofmans had two more children. Clara was born on January 7, 1902, and William was born on October 26, 1904. A. Cohen, known as "Auntie Cohen," the midwife for many babies in early Delray, helped deliver William. Anna possessed a deep repose and a reservoir of inner strength from which she drew her quiet lifestyle. Reared in a modest and conservative manner, the children grew to adulthood in the quiet village of Delray, nurtured by their parents' example and endurance.

The Hofman family in front of their home in 1909
Left to right: Anna, Willie, Annie, Adolf, and Clara

Delray, May 14, 1903

Dear Mother,

    At last the new addition to our house is almost finished. Mr. Hoenes, who built our two-story house seven years ago has as his foreman, John Thieme, our good friend from church in whom we have great confidence. As I wrote you, they are building a two-story wood frame addition to the back, or west, wall of our present house. The new space downstairs will have a large kitchen with a dining area. And, Mama, I am most pleased with the big walk-in pantry next to the eating area where I can store all my mason jars and baking utensils. The cool, dark pantry will also serve well for storing my jars filled with mango preserves and the tart jelly I make from green sea grapes. Flour, sugar, cereal grains, for all these, I will have more than enough storage. Adolf has ordered a large earthenware crockery pot to store drinking and cooking water in the pantry. It even has a spigot at the bottom so we can fill our drinking cups there in the pantry. The cool, dark pantry and earthenware will keep the water cool.

    Mr. Thieme measured the cooking area precisely some weeks ago so I could order a new indoor wood stove and oven from Mr. Sterling's catalog at the commissary and have it shipped by rail to Delray. There is even room for my Singer sewing machine beneath the north window, where I can see the men coming and going in the fields. Adolf says we must keep the old washtubs and hand wringer on the front porch, and I quite agree with him. Annie and I will need the easterly breezes as we work. And we certainly need the relief when boiling clothes over the big, three-legged iron pot.

    I am most intrigued, Mother, by the safe that Adolf has ordered. Since we live on the northern outskirts of town and have no neighboring houses within sight, we are sometimes visited by wandering bands of gypsies or hapless vagrants who follow the railroad tracks near our house. We need to secure the few valuables we have—a little cash, our immigration papers, and most important, our property deeds. Adolf went to West Palm Beach to purchase a small safe that he wants to hide under the floor in the pantry. He plans to saw out a section of the plank flooring in the pantry and lower the safe on its back so it lies on the ground with the padlock on the door facing up. That way we can get to it freely when needed. We will lay the planking section back in place and hide it with rag rugs that we can easily remove when needed. Nobody will ever notice the secret hiding place in the darkened pantry.

    Upstairs, the addition is large enough for two more bedrooms and a wide hallway. Mr. Hoenes and Mr. Thieme have yet to alter the stairs. Adolf wants the entry to the stairs reversed. In this way, we can enter the house through the side kitchen door and head straight for the stairs, and our dirt-caked shoes and clothes will not be dragged through the parlor. I have a garden filled with sweet potatoes and pole beans close to the house. Mother, the most frightening thing happened when I was working in the garden. My girls were playing in the shade of a nearby bush. I looked up and saw the most terrifying thing, a rattlesnake. I grabbed the hoe and ran over to the snake as it slithered toward Clara who was crawling toward the snake. I swung at the snake with all my might and sliced it in two. I grabbed Clara and held her close while I thanked the Lord for her safety.

Even though we risk such dangers, we are content here. Our house has almost doubled in size, and we continue to add new trees and plants to our property.

        Best wishes and love to all the family,
                      Anna

The Haden Mango

Adolf continued to experiment with a number of tropical fruits, including what is known today as the Haden mango. Captain John Haden arrived in Coconut Grove in 1896, just a few months after the railroad had been completed to Miami. Haden became interested in tropical fruits and started an experimental station. His specialty was mangoes. When he heard of a rare Mulgoba mango tree north of Delray that had withstood the great frost of 1895, Haden purchased some of the seeds and planted them in August of 1902. Even though he died the next January, his wife bravely cultivated the new trees for eight years before they began to bear fruit. The first fruit plucked from one of the trees weighed 22 ounces. Mrs. Haden sent two of these new mangoes to Washington to be registered as the Haden mango. Even though Adolf raised turpentine mangoes and other varieties in the early years, he preferred Haden mangoes and continued to plant and cultivate more and more of them in his groves.

Delray, July 19, 1903

Dear Father,

We are very happy with the goodness of this year's harvest. This year, however, the profit on our crops will be quite small. Our shipments of pineapples are only partly filled because this year once again, Cuba has the authority as it does from year to year to ship more and more pineapples to the United States with very little customs duty. Furthermore, we must pay up to two dollars to our workers for the produce they harvest. They in Cuba get anyone around willing to work for very little because the laborers need the work so badly.

I continue to add to my fruit trees. As a result of our common interest in experimenting with tropical fruits, I became friends with Captain John Haden of Coconut Grove years ago. He traveled everywhere in search of new and exotic things to grow. Last year, during one of his visits to the Delray area, he gave me some seeds from a rare variety of mango called Mulgoba. Captain Haden got his seeds from Eldridge Gale, who lives in Mangonia [later renamed Lake Worth], a small village north of Delray. Haden planted his Mulgoba seeds last year in hopes of developing a tastier mango. I, too, planted mine last year to experiment with this new type of mango and see how it would prosper. I hope to hear what will become of Haden's experiment also.

Always, I am eager to buy more land. The Model Land Company has many acres to offer, but at present, I am content to wait until I can acquire land adjacent to property I now own, and at a reasonable price. So I will wait and buy later this year.

We are quite happy and content, and also we are all in very good health. No matter how high the work prices are, I think we are still much better off here and have made more progress than we could have done in the North.

My very best greetings to all of you,
Adolf and family

The 1903 Hurricane
The Inchulva Disaster

Hurricanes sometimes struck the Delray area, leaving destruction and disaster in their wake. One of the most memorable storms was the 1903 hurricane. The National Weather Service indicates that the eye of the 1903 hurricane came on shore near Delray with winds estimated at 85 miles per hour. Mrs. John Blank, who was extremely ill with malaria, was alone in her house when the hurricane struck. During the height of the storm, the John Zill family noticed that the Blank house was being blown off its foundation. They hurried into the house, rescued Mrs. Blank, and brought her safely to their home. In addition to destroying houses and damaging property, the 1903 hurricane left a permanent legacy off shore.

Delray, September 13, 1903

Dear Mother,

Only a few days have passed since a terrible hurricane battered our coastline and caused great damage to Delray. The townspeople are still struggling to clean up the debris left in its wake. Our family suffered little damage from the hurricane's wind and rain save for torn tree limbs strewn around our grounds and floors soaked from water blowing in under the doors and window cracks.

Little warning we had except for the customary series of four blasts from the train whistle and then the final four long blasts, which at this time of year, signal an approaching storm. The series of warnings started as the train passed by Boca Raton some miles south of us. It gave us scant time to harbor the cows, horse, and mule inside the barn and fasten the doors.

The exciting news about a shipwreck was all over town. To our astonishment the storm battered a large steamship so violently that it was grounded just off our shoreline. A steamship named the S.S. Inchulva was on its way past Delray when the hurricane's force reached its peak. In the turmoil of winds and the lashing of the waves, the grounded ship broke into several pieces and sank just off shore.

In town, the news is that the Captain, the first mate, and two-thirds of the crew survived. They were helped by a party of Nassau Negroes who waved lanterns to signal survivors that they were within reach of the shore. Two men jumped overboard and swam to shore, where the Nassaus pulled the floundering men from the churning surf. The surviving shipmen and the captain were taken to the Inn, also known as the Chapman House, and there they remain under the good care of Mrs. Chapman. She dressed their deep cuts and nursed their wounds and watched over them through the night.

Other crewmen on board the Inchulva were not so fortunate. Nine men perished. Their bodies eventually washed to shore in the ocean swells and surging waves that pounded the shore. The bodies were reverently gathered and covered with canvas, and prayers were said to consecrate their deaths. The nine men were then buried in the high ridge of sand overlooking the ocean where the ship went down.

Everywhere in Delray there is a sense of excitement and urgency as people eagerly discuss the shipwreck and its survivors. Many curiosity seekers rushed to the beach the next few days. The girls and I, along with our new neighbors, Sophie Frey and her daughter Carrie, were among them. On the night the hurricane hit, Sophie and her children ran through the woods to our house, fearful that their little house by the canal would not survive the storm.

People scurried up and down the beach, exhilarated that such a calamity had hit our small village. A staggering sight lay before us. Splintered boards and floating lumber bobbed up and down in the surf. More timbers from the sunken ship were strewn every which way on the beach along with splintered crates and broken pieces of cargo. Bottles and coconuts were scattered up and down the beach along with the stinking bloated bodies of dead fish that washed ashore.

Everything was tangled in masses of twisted, stinking seaweed, but a stronger stench filled the air. Washing back and forth in the foam were sacks of wheat—torn apart—their contents rotting in the water. Much of the Inchulva's cargo was the wheat that washed ashore. The unbearable stench lingers up and down the beach and can even be smelled as far away as town, so strong is the odor.

What a wild and wind-battered beach. The sea grape branches were all but bare, stripped by gales of wind. Their saucer-shaped leaves lay scattered everywhere in careless heaps. Clumps of sea oats were bent sideways, flapping in the gusty winds. Piles of seaweed driven far back from the shoreline to the base of the dunes lay rotting in the sun.

Scattered everywhere were thousands of broken shells and bits of crushed coral stirred up from the ocean floor by the hurricane.

Onshore, not far from the churning waves, were large chunks of rubbery, spongelike ambergris, so it is named, or whale vomit, which washes up after a hurricane from far out at sea where the storm has taken its toll on the sea creatures. Everywhere, people were eagerly collecting the ambergris to ship north since people boast that it brings high prices for its use in making perfume.

We left the site of the wreck and the exhilaration of people still pulling lumber from the churning surf and gathering ambergris. Slowly, we headed north along the sand ridge where the clatter of palmetto leaves added to the sound of the waves.

As we headed for the canal and home, we walked along the old dune ridge, now overgrown with wild grass and sea oats, where rests the Orange Grove House of Refuge. Wistfully, I gazed at the forlorn place, "the stronghold of Zion set on a hill," and I longed for years gone by, for Annie Andrews and the fine friendship we shared at Zion. I saw the building's green paint trim, eaten by the years of acrid salt air, fallen in flakes on the wide veranda surrounding the house. Its shuttered doors are of no use to the survivors of the Inchulva *for its keepers have departed long ago. Yet my Zion still stands.*

My love to you and all the relatives,
Anna

In contrast to the great calamity of the 1903 hurricane was the warmth shared by friends in the small Delray community. Holidays provided a brief respite from the fields and a renewal of the spirit.

Delray, December 26, 1903

Dear Mother,

Even though this letter will reach you long after Christmas, I must tell you of the wonderful Christmas Eve we had this year as the guests of John and Margaret Wuepper. They are German Lutherans who arrived in Delray from Michigan this year. John lived alone in a tent near the Delray railway station for some time last year, determining whether or not to settle his family in Delray. Pleased with the plentiful sun and the promise of opportunity, he began building his house before sending for his family. They arrived this year with several other families from Bay City, Michigan. At last, the Wuepper house has been completed and faces Atlantic Avenue, the main street in town. The street is some nine feet in width, made mostly of rock and sand, and covered with a layer of crushed oyster shells.

After supper, Adolf read Luke's account of the birth of Christ from our old German Bible while Annie, baby Clara, and I listened. Annie, now eight years old, read aloud the prayer for Christmas Eve from my prayer book. After that, we left for the Christmas service and gathering at the Wuepper house.

My greatest delight was the tall balsam tree so much like the tannenbaum we had in Erpfingen. Mr. Wuepper lighted each small wax candle and was careful to keep a bucket of water next to the tree as is necessary. How lovely the tree was with its many paper chains and cookie ornaments that Mrs. Wuepper and her children had made. Even garlands of tinsel brought from the North glistened on the tree. They also had sparkling hand-blown balls of glass from the village of Lauscha in the Thuringian mountains north of Nürenberg. Since we had heard their tree was to be very special, I wrapped up some of the woven straw stars and snowflakes you sent me from Bavaria and gave them to the Wueppers as a Christmas gift and housewarming present. How delighted she was to see these ornaments from our fatherland.

All of us were much relieved to speak in German during the evening, for others attending were also Germans from Michigan, the Roth family, the Zill family, and the Blank family. Even though my English improves quite steadily in the eight years I have been in Delray, I am always thankful for company in the mother tongue. These fine people will greatly swell our small group of Lutherans at the kirche services in our home.

Later, we gathered around the tree and joined Mr. Wuepper in singing "Stille Nacht, Heilige Nacht," "Von Himmel Hoch," and other German hymns. The Wueppers even brought an organ with them when they moved, so indeed it was a true Christmas service for all of us.

Presents were given to Annie and Clara and to all the children there through the kindness of John, who traveled to Michigan to buy the large balsam Christmas tree and the presents. Later, we were treated to Mrs. Wuepper's Springerle cookies as well as her Pfeffernüssen. We were also served kuchen with raisins and sugar frosting as good as any of the best in all of Württemberg. She has a wood mold to press her Springerle dough in just as you do at home. Mrs. Zill brought her delicious Lebkuchen to share. The warmth of such wonderful people will certainly be welcome in this struggling town of Delray.

After Adolf untied the horse and buggy, we left and headed down the main street until we turned north on Bay Street. Finally, we reached the narrow, sand trail leading north to our home. A stiff evening breeze rustled the palmetto fronds and carried the sharp scent of salt air blown in from the ocean. Only the silver stars brightened our way home, reminding me of the flickering candles on the Wuepper tree and of the warmth of our Christmas together.

> Give my love to all the family,
> Anna

ACQUIRING ADDITIONAL FARMLAND

Adolf was primarily a farmer, a man trained by his family and agricultural college to cultivate and nurture the land. From his initial point of view, land was intended to yield food for his family and produce cash crops for marketing. Adolf's original sixty acres contained various types of soils that were well suited to different crops. The western parcel of his land lay on the old coastal ridge and consisted of white sandy soil and topsoil well adapted to the growing of pineapples. "Jack Rice and Mr. Tasker came about the same time. They and I set out the first pineapple fields" (Peebles, Interview with Adolf Hofman, 1937).

In contrast, Adolf's land that sloped eastward toward the shore of the canal was rich with muck, which nourished abundant vegetables such as eggplant, tomatoes, peppers, and beans. Hofman wanted to obtain more muck land to expand his vegetable crops, this time on the east side of the canal where he had already purchased five acres in 1903.

Adolf bought additional muck land east of the canal from Elnathan T. Field, who owned considerable tracts of land on the southeast coast of Florida. Field had been awarded this land by the State of Florida for his efforts at beautifying the coastal region to attract settlers. As early as 1883, Field had made three trips to Trinidad to secure coconuts to plant along the ocean front between Cape Florida and Hypoluxo. Hofman purchased seven and a half acres of this land east of the canal from Field's estate on May 10, 1905. Now Adolf owned even more fertile muck land bordering both sides of the canal.

Hofman continued to expand the farming potential of this muck land. Gradually, he bought all the land bordering the east side of the canal between Northeast Seventh Street and Northeast Fourth Street, specifically Lots 14 through 19. He later purchased the land adjacent to these lots known as the west half of Government Lot No.1. The east half of Government Lot No.1 housed the Orange Grove House of Refuge, and Adolf's west half contained the morass and muck along the canal. His area for raising vegetable crops more than tripled by all these purchases. Moreover, the Florida East Coast Canal narrowed somewhat near Hofman's property and afforded him quick and easy access to his farmland across the canal by means of his own narrow lighter.

Slowly, over the years, Adolf continued to acquire additional land to the west with the dream of extending his pineapple fields. He planted grapefruit and orange trees and various specimens of exotic fruit trees to produce additional produce for market. He steadily cultivated acres of mango trees and experimented with grafting various types of mango trees. Original deeds and land sale records reveal that Adolf also purchased ninety acres of land of Section 11 and Section 12, far to the west of Delray.

Delray, March 13, 1904

Dear Father,

This winter, we had pretty cold weather. In January we had a frost that destroyed all the delicate vegetables. Nonetheless, since it was still sunny here, we started a new planting. At this time of the year in

March, the weather is quite favorable for the growth of the plants, but it is very dry. Rain would be most welcome. From the look of things, we will have a very good harvest. Already I can start with picking tomatoes this week. I have been picking beans already for a few weeks. My only problems are that the prices are very low this year and the wages outrageous.

In November of last year, I bought and received the deed for more land adjacent to my present property. I bought five acres designated as Lots 16 and 17 from the Model Land Company for only $250. These lots are east of my sixty acres, just across the canal, and I can well use them for planting tomatoes and other vegetables in the fertile muck. For others, the land would be worthless because of the hosts of insects and mosquitoes that breed there. But for me, the moist soil is just what I need. I can easily reach it on my lighter, which I use to drag my mule across the canal for a full day of plowing. I am even more content here now that I own good farm property on both sides of the canal and can plant even more crops to sell. My plans are to purchase even more muck land on the east side of the canal.

The typhoid epidemic in our area was very severe this winter. Already people in Delray have died of this dreaded disease. I thank God my family and I have been spared.

With best greetings,
Yours, Adolf and family

Delray, June 21, 1904

Dear Mother,

Today a child was buried and my heart is heavy. What a dark spirit hangs over our townspeople. Our friends, the Zills and the Wueppers, have suffered a severe loss, and we grieve with them during their time of sorrow. Surely they have had more than their share of sorrow in losing three of their family members.

It has been a bleak time in Delray with malaria and typhoid fever taking their toll. The mosquitoes were unusually bad last year, breeding in any standing water. Thus many people contracted diseases. The constant monotonous droning of the mosquitoes persists in my ears.

It was tragedy enough when both Henry and Clara Roth died last year of typhoid fever, but to have their only child, their two-year-old son who survived them, perish of jaundice meant the end of their small family. John and Margaret Wuepper, the boy's aunt and uncle, along with his grandparents, the John Zills, had been caring for him in their homes from the time his parents died. Over the course of several weeks, the little boy's skin slowly turned a grayish yellow, and he was unable to keep any food in his frail body. Day after day, he languished and became increasingly listless as his skin muddied and darkened. Margaret, Clara's sister, was with him at his last moment. Just before he died, he lifted his tiny arms and cried, "Mama, Mama," for his dead mother. To think of it, all three in one family perished in just two years.

The Zills asked Mr. Sterling and Kemp Burton to make the coffin as they usually do for those departed, but this time, it was a small, sad coffin for the withered boy. Along with our German Lutheran friends who worship with us, many of our townspeople came to the funeral held in the Zill home. John Zill read from the Holy Bible, and all the children gathered around the coffin and sang one of our hymns, "Let Me Depart Peacefully."

What was harder to bear was the procession to the old Bay Ridge graveyard, located on the steep sand of the beach ridge. The boy's relatives wanted him buried there beside his parents instead of in the new Pine Ridge Cemetery in town.

The trip across the canal on the town lighter was treacherous. Men had to balance the pitifully small coffin on planks so they could maneuver the crossing. Then began the mournful trek north to Laing Street where the boundary of the cemetery is located. We trudged through the sand and climbed the ridge east of Andrews Avenue. There we came to rest amid the saw palmettos and salt spray while we looked down at the tiny coffin sadly braving the wind and sea.

The final prayers were said, the body was committed to the grave, and we sang the final hymn, "Command Your Ways, Oh Lord." I wove a small cross out of a dried palmetto frond to place on the plain coffin so the boy would not go barren into the ground. As the box was slowly lowered, we turned our faces and wept. We left in silence and began the slow journey home, I carrying our new child stirring in my body these five months.

My love to you,
Anna

Religious Life

Religion played a large role in the lives of the Hofmans. Adolf and Anna were faithful to their Christian beliefs proclaimed by the Evangelical Lutheran Church, the faith they had shared in Germany. As Anna's letter dated Oct. 5, 1898, reveals, they held regular family worship services in their home. In 1898 Rev. Edward Fischer, a Lutheran minister in central Florida, assumed the responsibility of seeking out Lutherans along the east coast of Florida. He contacted Adolf and began conducting Lutheran worship services in German twice a year in the Hofman home. Other German Lutherans attended these services as they settled in the area. These included the John Zill family, the Henry Roth family, the John Blank family, and the John Wuepper family. After the arrival of the Wuepper family in 1903, plans for constructing a church building got under way when Margaret Wuepper insisted that she and the children would return to Michigan unless a church was constructed. In 1903 and 1904 religious services alternated between the Hofman, Zill, and Wuepper homes until the church building was completed. They sometimes worshiped on the Wuepper porch and more often in the Zill home, which was the largest house.

In 1904 Adolf served on the original building committee for the first wooden church edifice, which still stands, relocated behind Trinity's present sanctuary on North Swinton Avenue. Adolf also served as one of the original church trustees and sang regularly in the church choir. Over the years Anna was a member of the Ladies Aid Society, and both she and Adolf contributed financial support to special church needs and building projects. They helped to beautify the old church building by contributing a stained glass window after the sanctuary was remodeled in 1938.

The frame structure of Trinity Evangelical Lutheran Church was under construction late in 1904. (Courtesy of Trinity Lutheran Church Archives)

Delray, October 16, 1904

Dear Mother,

Today is the first Sunday we worshiped in our new church building and dedicated it to the glory of God. Finally, after several years of worshiping in our house, John Zill's house, and John Wuepper's porch, we have our church built, thanks mainly to Margaret Wuepper, who told her husband she would not stay in Delray unless a church was built. The Wueppers even donated an organ that Mr. Sterling had on sale for fifteen dollars. It is placed in the front corner of the church by the hymnal board. We even have an organist, young Laura Zill, who is only twelve years old. What a fine job she did today playing it.

The men have been constructing our church on the southeast corner of Boynton Avenue and Lowry Street ever since August. Our church is a wood frame building with a steep pitched roof and many windows. It is approximately twenty-two feet wide, fifty feet long, and twelve feet high. Adolf was elected to the building committee along with Mr. C. H. Miller and Mr. Wuepper. The three of them will continue to serve as Trustees of the church as well. After much discussion in a meeting, the men voted to name the congregation *Evangelische Lutherische Dreieinigkeits Gemeinde* (Trinity Evangelical Lutheran Congregation).

They bought the land from Mr. Blackmer for the amount of seventy-five dollars. Mr. Blackmer even donated half the cost back to the congregation. What a time our few members had raising the nine hundred fifty dollars needed to cover the land and building costs, considering the hard times. Help, however, came from Mr. Flager, who contributed one hundred dollars toward the construction costs.

We have our own pastor, Reverend Frederick Pebler, who was officially called by the men and placed by the Synod to serve our congregation. He brought his sister, Miss Hermine Pebler, to keep house for him. What a lovely voice she has. Soon we can even start our own choir, which I know Adolf will want to join.

Trinity Evangelical Lutheran Church was originally located on the corner of Boynton Avenue and Lowry Street. Henry Flagler donated $100 toward the building's construction as was his practice for new churches.

Adolf was happy to get a seat by a window where he could keep an eye on his horse and buggy so no one would bother them while they were tied to a post outside. We have no pews yet. Instead, we sat on wide benches that have no backs.

But some things do not change even in the new country, Mother. As is the custom in Germany, all the men sit on the left side, and all the women sit on the right side of church, and as usual, the men always go to communion first. Margaret Wuepper fashioned a lovely Klingelbeutel for collecting the money, complete with a large, deep bag made of rich red velvet. At the bottom of the bag, she fastened a long, thick golden tassel. Her husband attached the velvet bag to a thin pole long enough to reach to the end of every bench in order to collect the contributions. The jangling bell at the end of the pole will surely awaken any sleeping parishioners and inattentive dreamers.

In a meeting early in October, the Elders decided to rent a small house near the church building until the church was completed. The house will be used to hold classes for the religious instruction of our children. In the mornings, the children are to attend public school, and from one to four in the afternoons, they are to receive instruction in the German language and in Luther's Small Catechism from Pastor Pebler. It is to be called the Deutsche Schule (German School), and Annie will attend it when Pastor Pebler is able to get it established. The Zill and Wuepper children will also join her.

At last, our own church! How I thank God for our house of worship. We have a lovely altar and altar linens as well as a fine crucifix. The wall behind the altar is adorned with the Christian symbols of a cross and a communion chalice. How I love this building already. At last—our own place of worship in Delray. It gave me great comfort to go to this building and enter God's sanctuary. It is a relief from the drudgery of the fields and the bleak sameness of every day. How my long pregnancy wears me down. Here I can rest beside still waters and restore my soul. Here I can come to meditate and find a refuge. This church will be my sacred spot in this village—my second Zion.

>Your loving daughter,
>Anna

The original church structure was moved across town to North Swinton Avenue in 1965, and still stands behind the present sanctuary of Trinity Evangelical Lutheran Church.

*Children from the **Deutsche Schule** (the German School) line up on the church steps of Trinity Evangelical Lutheran church with their hats and lunch baskets on September 12, 1905. The children identified in the top row are Clara Wuepper Miller (left) and Annie Hofman (right). Seated below Clara is Margie Wuepper Lang. One of the boys is Rudy Wuepper, and the other boys belong to the Zill family. Written on the three slates are the words "Deutsche Schule, Delray, Florida, September 12, 1905."*

This photograph of Trinity Evangelical Lutheran Church in 1904 illustrates that the parishioners sat on wooden benches without backs. The front pews were reserved for the Elders and Trustees. In keeping with German tradition, the men sat on one side, and the women sat on the other side.

Delray, December 8, 1904

Dear Mother,

How happy I am to share more news about our newborn, who as you know, was born on October 26, 1904. Although we call him Willie, he was officially baptized Wilhelm Adolf Hofman on Sunday, December 4, some five and a half weeks after he was born.

We are excited that he was the first baby baptized in our new church. We are thankful that Willie remains in good health after an uncomplicated delivery, thanks to the help of "Auntie" Cohen. She was the midwife at his birth, just as she has been for so many babies in Delray. We are grateful for her services, and already we have received Willie's official birth certificate bearing her signature.

The girls were quite excited when Adolf hitched the horse and buggy, and they helped me dress Wilhelm in the baptismal gown and cap you made for Annie's baptism in Germany. The embroidered edges are still as full and lovely as when you made them, but I must confess that, even though I kept them carefully packed in my steamer trunk upstairs, they are spotted over the years with a few yellow stains from the humid climate we have here. The girls and I crowded into the buggy with Willie, and Adolf headed for church less than a mile away.

During the church service, Wilhelm's baptism went as planned without a single cry or whimper when Pastor Pebler poured the water on his head. The new baptismal font is quite serviceable and attractive. How good it was to have my dear brother Paul

A group of friends gathered at the Hofman home following Willie's baptism on December 5, 1904. Front row: Clara (second from left), Annie (third from left), Anna holding Willie (seated) Back row: Adolf (third from right)

journey all the way from Erpfingen to be with us and serve as godfather and witness. Adolf was just as happy to have his brother Gustav travel from Mönchhof to be witness and serve as godfather also.

It was a good plan for Gustav and Paul to meet in Stuttgart and travel to Bremen to make the long voyage; they had an easier time of it. It's a good thing the Florida East Coast Railway has a daily train passing through Delray. Our depot is forever busy and cluttered with shipping fresh fruits and vegetables to the North, especially during the winter season. They were amazed at the flurry of activity surrounding the station and the great number of crates being shipped from Delray.

After the service, we headed for home with a number of friends, including Sophie Frey, the Betzes, the Wueppers, and Pastor Pebler, where we feasted on a huge meal that included my creamed potatoes and creamed spinach. Adolf even arranged for Mr. Muller, the town photographer, to photograph all of us for this special occasion. After the photographs were taken, the women headed indoors to clean up the dishes while the men headed to the fields, where Adolf was proud to show them his fruit trees and vegetables he has labored so hard to cultivate. He is quite pleased with Germania Plantation, for so he calls it, and Paul and Gustav eagerly took in the sights of so much tropical vegetation.

They were astonished at the variety of exotic tropical plants growing in the middle of winter, no less. The guava trees, with their smooth, mottled bark and dark green leaves, impressed them. More fascinating to them were the enormous, towering mango trees just bursting into bloom. They were early this year. Each tree glistened with new sprouts of shiny, wine-colored leaves topped with thousands of small yellow buds just beginning to blossom on every branch and stem. The pungent fragrance of so many budding trees proved quite intoxicating and almost overpowered our brothers as they lingered in the grove, inhaling the heady aroma.

Next, they rambled through the dense rows of banana palms. They marveled at how smooth and thick the trunks were and how gracefully the leaves spread like a swaying cover of green fans rustling in the afternoon breeze that swept across the fields.

Leaving the deep thicket of banana trees, the men marched through rows and rows of beans, eggplant, and tomatoes in order to reach the railroad tracks. They climbed over the tracks and continued farther west to the land we own beyond the tracks. Here, acres of pineapple spikes rose to greet them. Their thick stalks pierced the sky with serrated points in endless rows stretching across the horizon. Adolf explained how pineapples are grown from slips or the crown cut from ripe pineapples. He also told them about the thick protective boots and gloves the cutters have to wear to protect themselves from the spines on the pineapple leaves.

Late in the afternoon, as they headed back, Adolf led them through the grove of avocado trees, the fruit of which we commonly call "alligator pears," much to Paul's amusement. The wild pawpaws sprouting here and there also intrigued them.

Home to us in the twilight, our brothers expressed their awe once more about the exotic trees and crops Adolf has tended so methodically. No doubt Paul will have more things to tell you about our way of living in the wilds of Delray.

Best wishes and love to everyone,
Anna

Anna was dressed in her Sunday best and Willie wore the family baptismal gown for this photograph taken in late December 1904.

Even in its early years, Delray was known for its racial and ethnic diversity. The small town drew all sorts of residents and workers who steadily made Delray the agricultural center of what was to become Palm Beach County.

Delray, May 7, 1906

Dear Mother,

    Today Adolf hitched up the horse and buggy and took the girls and me on an excursion that we are not likely to forget. We headed south to Atlantic Avenue, then turned west and rode slowly through town since Annie so loves seeing people and the activity going on in town, especially by the railroad station. We reached the Palm Beach-Miami Appian Way, for so the Flagler people have labeled the county rock road running by the Chapman House. So grand a name for so narrow a road! We then turned south and rode parallel to the train tracks for some miles to visit a small colony of immigrants who settled south of Delray two years ago.

    Mother, can you believe that Japanese settlers have come here from halfway around the world? They have named their small colony Yamato, which I am told is the ancient sacred name for Japan. The great railroad titan and land promoter, Mr. Flagler, assured them land and brought them here. He had to obtain permission from the Emperor of Japan before his subjects could leave the country, and even then, Flagler had to guarantee that they would own land before the emperor would allow them to emigrate.

Flagler, of course, wants to bring in more skilled farmers and vegetable growers to swell the population of South Florida and encourage others to settle here. Of course, it will fatten his freight profits as well. Thus Flagler's Model Land Company brought some twenty-five men from Japan and located the colony south of Delray in 1904.

Today, Adolf introduced me to Jo Sakai, the founder of the Yamato Colony. Sakai spent almost a year securing the young men, most of whom are still single. They are from the vicinity of his native town, Miyazu, Japan, and they emigrated in hopes of establishing a permanent colony here. Since their arrival, they have worked hard to establish a foothold on the flatlands south of town.

Annie, Clara, and Willie were delighted when we had to take off our shoes, for such is the Japanese custom, before entering one of their small dwellings so unlike any of our houses in Delray. Adolf followed Jo Sakai to the fields, eager to ask about the unique Japanese ways of planting and cultivating crops. Mr. Sakai was quick to respond, even though, as always, the language barrier caused problems and led to some laughter on both parts. How good it was to hear Adolf laugh. We also met George Morikami, only nineteen years old, who had recently arrived from Miyazu to join the colony.

Mama, the Japanese are only some of the different people and nationalities we have living together in our area, people you would never find living in Germany. Of course there are the Anglo-Americans who came here with Adolf or worked on the railroad crews as the roadbed and tracks were being laid. Many of them are now shopkeepers in town and do quite well.

You would be amazed by the Seminoles from the Everglades who camp in the area near Lake Ida. They wander into town and gather around the stores, anxious to look through the catalogs and goods. They are a strong and silent people with dark features and colorful clothes and beads. They seem to visit town at frequent intervals and are attracted by the shops and activity along Atlantic Avenue.

More people you will not see in Erpfingen are our Negro residents, a goodly number of them. Some of them actually lived in the area before Adolf and Mr. Linton arrived. Some of these original settlers were newly freed slaves, and some intermarried with Seminoles. A Bahamian family from Bimini settled in Delray three years after we arrived. Years ago, the Negroes built two churches, and they already have their own schoolhouse and teacher. One of the residents, Mr. Cole, is employed by Adolf and works many long hours in the pineapple fields together with John Eggers.

You would be interested to know that more Germans arrive regularly. In fact, together with Frank Haller, Paul Grootman and his wife purchased acreage immediately south of our sixty acres. The Grootmans built a home on their property and are quite sociable. In fact, every third Saturday, Paul Grootman sets up a keg of beer on his grounds and invites everyone he knows to join him for the afternoon. I can hear the noise and laughter clear to our house, and I suspect the Anglo ladies are somewhat suspicious of these German beer parties and look somewhat askance at us German ladies. Perhaps they also disapprove of the German school our children attend every afternoon.

*German settlers in Linton and Delray were proud of their ethnic identity. Church services and lessons in the German school were conduct in German for many years. Students in the **Deutsche Schule** display their slates. Left to right: Otto Zill, Elmer Zill, Emil Zill, Annie Hofman, Maggie Zill Weber, Caroline Wuepper Smith, and Mary Zill Putnam. Annie Hofman is the only child wearing shoes in this picture.*

Even though we Germans are talked about for our language and customs, we get in our laughs, too. One time Adolf lent his mule to Mr. Hall so he could plow his land over by the canal. Mr. Hall returned the mule, complaining that when he tried to plow, the mule would not budge.

"I know mules are stubborn," he said, "but this dumb mule is the laziest and most stubborn mule I've ever seen."

Adolf simply replied, "Oh no, this is a hardworking mule, but he only understands German. You've got to speak German to this mule."

Mr. Hall answered, "Well, I'm not about ready to learn a new language just to talk to some dumb mule."

As you can see, Mother, we have quite a mixture of races and nationalities here in the little village of Delray. Although we still struggle with English at times, it must be much more difficult for the newly arrived residents of Yamato. I hear that, with Mr. Flagler's help and encouragement, they have already built a small train station for shipping their produce.

How different for you at home, Mama, with all the relatives surrounding you and friends so close. Although I miss all of you dearly, I have grown to admire the new faces and customs that mix here in Delray.

                          Your loving daughter,
                          Anna

Delray's Racial and Ethnic Diversity

From its beginnings, Delray had a harmonious racial and ethnic diversity that helped create a strong sense of community. When Linton made his first visit to the area in 1894, about fourteen African-American families were already living as farmers and fishermen. Fagan Henry and his wife Jane Monroe led Negro families from the Florida panhandle between 1890 and 1896. They persuaded relatives and friends from Gadsden County in northwest Florida to join them. Former tenant farmers and workers, who came here because of Florida's homesteading policy, settled west of town and bought land there from Flagler's Model Land Company. Many of the blacks who migrated from the Deep South, the Bahamas, and South Dade County, found work building the railroad bed or laying rails as the railway expanded south to Linton in 1896. Some brought their families and made their homes in Linton. The black families were eager to educate their children, and they petitioned the Dade County School Board to assign them a teacher and administrator. Mr. B.F. James was sent to their community to be the first teacher in 1896. Linton's first church, the Mt. Olive Missionary Baptist Church, was built in 1896. In 1897 black settlers organized Mt. Tabor, now the St. Paul African Methodist-Episcopal Church. The first black family from Bimini settled in Linton in 1898. Among the early black families were the Monroes, Cohens, Coles, Chambers, Simms, Brights, Campbells, Smiths, Bellamys, Muses, and Newmans.

Many of the earliest settlers were from Germany or of German ancestry. They were hardworking farmers and shopkeepers who wanted to preserve their customs and language as well as learn English and blend into the community. Two industrious Germans, John Zill and John Wuepper, opened a general store in 1906 that was a combination grocery, meat market, and dry goods store. The store became a popular center for local residents and drew all sorts of colorful characters. Local gator hunters brought their alligator skins to the store to ship them North. One time, they tricked Laura Zill into eating alligator meat by telling her it was fish. Besides the Hofmans, Wueppers, and Zills, other early German settlers included the Roths, the Blanks, the Millers, and the Freys.

Japanese workers from the Yamato colony wait for the Florida East Coast Railway train to ship their produce north. The Yamato railroad station was constructed with the help of Henry Flagler. (Courtesy of Delray Beach Historical Society)

The Yamato Colony

Adding to the diversity were the Japanese settlers in the Yamato colony just south of Delray. They were highly respected for their unique farming methods characterized by the patient cultivation of small plots of land. They took great pride in their work and were meticulous farmers. As diligent laborers, they complemented the hardworking farmers of other races and helped create a communal work ethic. The Japanese settlers regularly participated in Delray's civic and social life, and their children attended school with the whites.

An early description of the Yamato colony is found in a promotional booklet printed in 1906 by the Florida East Coast Railway. "Yamato is a Japanese colony now consisting of only about twenty-five persons. They have been established two years and are making satisfactory progress in the cultivation of pineapples and vegetables. This is the vanguard of what the promoters, prominent Japanese gentlemen, hope to make a permanent settlement in Florida. Permission must be obtained from the Emperor of Japan before his subjects can leave the country, and even then they must be able to show tat they own land at the point to which they may be destined. Yamato is the original name of Japan."

Delray Farmers and the Florida East Coast Railway

Although Flagler's railway, which linked Delray to the northern markets, promised to be a blessing at first, it later proved otherwise to the farmers. The railway escalated competition with the Cuban pineapple market. After the Spanish-American War, the United States removed the tariff on Cuban pineapples to bolster Cuba's economy, and the railway cashed in on this new policy.

Adolf criticized the railway for controlling market prices and levying heavy freight charges on South Florida farmers. Matters grew worse after 1912 when the Florida East Coast Railway used steamer ferries carrying freight cars to bring Cuban pineapples to Key West and ship them by express rail direct to northern cities. As the years progressed, freight costs for local farmers and the railway's blatant patronage of the Cuban pineapple market curtailed Hofman's profits time and time again as noted repeatedly in various letters through the years.

Adolf Hofman
Grower of
Fancy Fruits and Vegetables
Germania Plantation

Delray, July 10, 1909

Dear Brother Fritz,

I find the time to write again at last. I have always been so busy that I was glad to get done with the necessary business correspondence. Indeed, as the saying goes, "one has much shearing and little wool" here, for this year and the last ones were the worst we have had here.

Salaries, fertilizers, and other costs continue to increase, and the products bring such a bad price that it is hardly worth it to ship them. From Delray alone, six to ten freight cars of tomatoes and pineapples were shipped daily for the past four months. The railroad company charges such high freight costs that the farmer has hardly any profit left. For instance, I had to pay $350 for a freight car full of cabbage to New York.

As long as there is no competing railroad, the railroads will continue to be run by the government, and things will not improve. But for both of these, there is not much hope since the railroad companies and the trust companies are America's worst robber barons. Even our ex-President Roosevelt, who tried to fight them with all his power, could not win against them.

Another terrible thing is the competition with Cuba. There, rich American corporate owners have bought up land and planted thousands of acres with pineapples and oranges in order to sell the fruit themselves in America. They have the advantage over us. They have cheaper and better land, cheaper labor, cheaper transportation costs, and very little fertilizer costs.

America was actually flooded with Cuban pineapples this year, and here in Florida we also had an exceptionally large crop. This year I shipped about 2,500 crates of pineapples, which would have fetched over $6,000 eight or ten years ago. This year I had to be satisfied with $1,600, which barely covers my expenses. With tomatoes I haven't done much better. Only with beans did I have a small profit.

The railroad and express companies have taken in $6,000 in freight costs from me alone. According to my estimate, that comes to over a half million dollars they've collected from Delray and the surrounding area. You can see how we poor farmers are being exploited by these robbers. To get rid of their excess money, they are extending the railroad to Key West, which has swallowed up millions of dollars. And for this, we poor farmers have to bleed.

With my family all is well, and I haven't had to spend a cent for a doctor so far. My eldest daughter had her confirmation this year although she is only thirteen years old. Only three were confirmed in our small German congregation.

        Greeting you and your dear family,
             Your brother,
                Adolf

Annie's confirmation in 1909 was an important event in the Hofman family. The church was beautifully decorated with palms and tropical plants for Palm Sunday. Left to right: Caroline Wuepper Smith, Annie Hofman, Margaret Zill Weber

After her mother's death in 1909, Anna wrote letters to her sisters in Erpfingen. Her letters convey the universal human threads of weddings and other family happenings.

Delray, September 10, 1910

Dear Pauline,

The girls and I, along with Adolf, went to a beautiful wedding today at the home of our good friend Sophie Frey. The occasion was the marriage of her daughter Carrie to William Zill. Having the ceremony in her home was a fine tribute to all the work and love that Sophie and her children have put into that old Luhrs house. Everyone who had flowers or ferns brought filled baskets early in the morning to help decorate the front room for the wedding that evening.

First, let me tell you about the surprise wedding shower the ladies gave Carrie and Will. William placed the engagement ring on Carrie's finger on June 22, under the trees where he first kissed her. The ladies in town have been dying to surprise her with a shower, so on August 27, we assembled all of our gifts, knowing that Carrie would be gone from her place. Will and Carrie spent the day over on the ocean ridge with a book and a picnic lunch and arrived home late that afternoon.

When they arrived, there was a large crowd of ladies and young girls settled on the lawn. Mrs. Burd took Will and Carrie by the arm and placed them in the center of the crowd, putting a large wash basket of presents before them. Carrie said she never knew she had so many friends and was very thankful for all the gifts she received to help her set up housekeeping in her own home. Laura Zill, Clara Wuepper, and Ada Godbold served ice cream and cake, which is a real treat we seldom have. John Zill, the meat cutter from Zill and Wuepper's store, is accustomed to ordering meat packed in ice, so he ordered ice cream carefully packed in ice to be brought down by train from West Palm Beach.

Annie and Clara were up early today, excited about attending the ceremony. The girls have been watching Carrie sew her own wedding gown from week to week on that old sewing machine Sophie brought with her to Linton years ago. Mrs. Cathcart, who is like a mother to many of the young girls in town, has the dry goods store in town. She helped Carrie choose a very pale sky blue, almost ice blue, silk batiste for the wedding gown.

Good thing that Carrie is an excellent seamstress because the dress required a great deal of detail work. The bodice was decorated with rows of pin tucks, and between each row of pin tucks, there was a one-inch lace insert. The long skirt was full, and near the bottom there were pin tucks with lace inserts. At the very bottom, there was a circle of lace three inches wide. The back of the dress had a row of buttons made of seed pearls, and the dress had full "leg o'mutton" sleeves. Above the bodice, near the neck, was a square yoke made of net, and surrounding the neck was a beautiful collar of fine lace.

Sophie sent to West Palm Beach for the bridal bouquet made of white roses. Ada Godbold, the bridesmaid, had a most unusual bouquet of white water lilies. The Frey boys, Willie and George, went west of town to Lake Ida early in the morning when the water lilies opened and picked more than a dozen of the native water lilies that grow wild in Lake Ida. The girls braided the long stems with pale blue ribbon and made the flowers into a lovely bouquet for Ada to carry.

As I said, at eight o'clock that morning, Ada and Doris Crego, who were in charge of the decorating, met the ladies at the door with their ferns and flowers sent to decorate the front room where the wedding was going to be held. Annie, Clara, and I also brought baskets of our flowers and asparagus fern. With the help of Willie and George, everyone finished decorating the room about noon. We brought over chairs from our house across the fields to help with the seating. Toward evening, Carrie's Uncle Cornelius went to town to get the cake and ice cream on special order from Zill and Wuepper's store.

Carrie began to dress about six o'clock. When she was finished, Sophie and Mrs. Cathcart pinned orange blossoms in her hair. She was beautiful and so happy. About seven o'clock the guests began to arrive. We were helping with the last-minute details when the first guests to arrive were Mrs. Kahn, her daughter Eva, and Nellie Fenno. Then came the Wuepper family; next, the John Zill family, followed by many others until the front room was filled and some had to stand.

The time came for the ceremony to begin. Rev. Arno Thieme from our church conducted the service. It was a lovely ceremony, and Annie and Clara were touched to see the wedding of their friend. Following the ceremony, the couple cut the wedding cake, and we helped serve the cake and ice cream out on the lawn. Soon it was over, and Carrie and Will left on the wagon to a new life in a home of their own.

The girls and I will never forget Carrie's beautiful gown and those lovely white water lilies from Lake Ida.

Greetings and love to all of you,
Your sister, Anna

As neighbors and fellow homesteaders, the Hofman and Frey families remained close friends through the years. Here they pose near the old Frey home down by the canal, north of the city limits. Left to right: Margarete Frey, William Frey, Annie Hofman, Sophie Frey

Agriculture was the mainstay of Linton and early Delray. Packing and shipping produce from Delray became a thriving business. The tomato packing house run by the Milton boys offered a lively diversion for the young people in town. The girls wrapped the tomatoes, and the boys made crates. Chase and Co., another big broker and packer, had a wooden structure alongside the railroad tracks. The biggest social event in early Delray was the grand opening of the Delray Canning Company in 1904.

Delray had a thriving packing and shipping industry. The sign on the wall reads, "Delray Growers and Packers Association." Annie Hofman is the first girl on the left in the back row.

Delray, May 4, 1911

Dear Sister Mathilde,

    Annie is over at the packing house downtown by the railroad tracks today. She's been packing tomatoes there for several weeks with her friends, Margaret and Leona, and I suspect that's the real reason she wants to be there. It can't be the money since the packing plant pays only five cents a box. The girls wrap the tomatoes in thin sheets of paper, and some of the faster workers can earn up to five dollars a day for their work. With Annie, it's more the sociability. She always needs someone to talk to. Besides, it's something to keep the young people busy after school and on Saturdays, and most of them ride their bicycles down there and have a good time of it.

    How long it will last, who can say? The local farmers bring the tomatoes to the packing house to ship north on consignment. But they take their chances. At times, tomatoes bring a good price because the market is just right, but more than likely, the farmers get word that the market is flooded with tomatoes again or hear some other excuse, according to the whims of the buyers. So there is very little profit for the farmers. That's why Adolf keeps his men busy in his own packing house using lots of excelsior to keep the tomatoes from bruising as the workers pack them. From there, Adolf takes them directly to the freight station and ships them north himself even though the freight costs more that way.

    Right now, Adolf is over west of Dixie Highway, shooting quail. I thought I would fix some roasted quail for supper, and he was headed west of the tracks anyway.

He wanted to look over the new fields he and his men planted. Now that the pineapples aren't as large as they use to be, he's planted other crops and a windbreak of sugar cane to protect them.

But he's got another notion in his head. He thinks that Delray will expand and grow north, especially now that it is incorporated as a town. He is even thinking of selling some of the old farmland as house lots once the move heads north. I told him Delray is not likely to come this direction, but he insists that the town is growing. I've reminded him we don't even have roads or streets coming through our property, but he claims that when the land is platted, we can make a good profit. True, he's already had his fair share of success with buying land and renting properties.

Before Adolf headed west of the tracks, I told him to cut down and strip some sugar cane stalks, so I could start boiling them with some guavas. I told Annie to come right home from the packing plant today since I need her and Clara to help me make guava jelly. I tried making preserves from the fruit of the loquat trees, but it was not half as good. This time, I'm sticking to the guava jelly, which always comes out good. I usually squeeze in a little fresh lime juice to keep the sugar cane from making the guavas too sweet. I suppose Adolf and Annie will be here soon, so I had better close.

> Best wishes from your sister,
> Anna

Annie holds a palm branch on the Hofman property.

Community Involvement and the Bank of Delray

As Delray grew, Adolf remained an active force in the town's development. Increasingly, he became involved in civic activities that promoted the improvement of the community. His proximity to Dade Avenue, later renamed Federal Highway, led tourists to stop frequently to purchase bushels of fresh fruit. At

Annie appears in a sun hat next to boxes of fruit on the front porch. Delray native, Dorothy Susleck, granddaughter of pioneer settler Sophie Frey, remembers how hard Annie worked loading up a wheelbarrow and pushing it to Federal Highway to sell fruit to tourists day after day.

times, his daughter Annie set a wheelbarrow filled with fruit by the road to attract more buyers. In this way, the Hofmans got to know many tourists from all over, some of whom returned year after year and even settled in Delray. Through his expanding sales and fruit shipments, Adolf became a well-known personality around town. He mingled with the packers, shippers, railroad clerks, and town merchants. As the years passed, Adolf continued to graft more and more mango and citrus trees until the immediate acres surrounding his house were filled with large groves.

During the years he was expanding his citrus and mango groves, Adolf became involved with a number of Delray men in a huge financial undertaking in 1912. On April 10, 1912, the following men applied to the State of Florida for a charter to incorporate the Bank of Delray: J.L. Troup, J.R. Cason, George J. Strickland, J.M. Cromer, and Adolf Hofman. The capital was set at $25,000 divided into 150 shares. The corporation was to exist for a term of ninety-nine years. The first annual meeting was held on the second Tuesday in January of 1913. Hofman took thirty shares of stock and became one of the Directors of the Bank of Delray.

The bank voluntarily provided double protection for its depositors by building its surplus and undivided profits in a reserve fund greater than the capital. It claimed to be the only bank in Palm Beach County where deposits were insured. In 1914 the Bank of Delray loaned Abraham George $1,500, the largest loan the bank ever made, which enabled him to build his large clothing store on the corner of Southeast Fourth Avenue and Atlantic Avenue. Abraham George became a highly respected businessman, and his popular store remained a favorite Delray landmark for over eight decades.

Adolf helped organize the Bank of Delray in 1912. It claimed to be the only fully insured bank in Palm Beach County. Mr. J. L. Troup, President, stands proudly in the lobby. (Courtesy of Delray Beach Historical Society)

By 1924 the Bank of Delray had become the Delray Bank and Trust Co. Adolf's son, William, was employed as a bookkeeper in 1924 and was appointed assistant cashier from 1925 to 1928. Later, during the Crash and subsequent banking failures when the Delray Bank and Trust Co. closed, Adolf, along with the other bank directors, was assessed to pay back the depositors.

In addition to his venture into banking, Adolf also involved himself in other civic matters over the years. He was one of the directors of the Delray Improvement Association, serving as treasurer in 1912 and 1913. As part of this organization, Adolf contributed to the expansion of Delray by promoting general property sales and land development. He stimulated the town's growth even more by platting some of his own land for sale in 1913. This plat was called the Hofman Addition, which made lots available for neighborhood houses and expanded Delray's city limits to the north.

In 1925 Adolf added to Delray's growth and economy once again. He was the motivating force behind the construction of the Arcade Building on Atlantic Avenue. The large building stimulated Delray's economic growth by attracting additional businesses and shoppers to downtown Delray.

During all these years, Adolf continued to be an active leader at Trinity Evangelical Lutheran Church. He remained one of the trustees of the church well into the late 1920s and remained an active congregation member until his death.

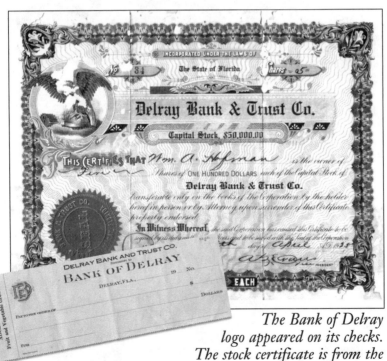

The Bank of Delray logo appeared on its checks. The stock certificate is from the Delray Bank & Trust Co., successor to the Bank of Delray.

Annie, Willie, Clara, and Anna pose in front of one of their mango trees on the way to the 1913 County Fair held in Delray.

County Fairs were a colorful relief from daily routine. Delray was considered the agricultural leader of Palm Beach County and hosted many of these fairs.

Delray, March 20, 1913

Dear Sister Pauline,

    We just received today's copy of the West Palm Beach newspaper, the *Tropical Sun*, which lists the prizes won at the recent Palm Beach County Fair held at Delray. The County Fair has been held here several times since Delray produces by far the largest and best crops in all the area, an accomplishment that

As the agricultural center of Palm Beach County, Delray was the scene of many County Fairs. They were the highlight of a productive agricultural year and the largest community social event of the year.

gives us great pride. What a treat to see so many of our friends' names in the paper. Delray residents won many of the prizes.

This was the County Fair I wrote you about earlier, the one where Willie planned to exhibit his rabbits for the first time. He has been raising them and caring for them for such a long time that we thought it was time for him to enter them in the fair now that he is almost nine years old.

He helped the girls pack the pineapples, bananas, and other fruit we always put on display at the county fairs. We loaded up the wagon early in the morning because Clara and Annie wanted to be there early enough to arrange Adolf's large vegetable display. They said they had a special way to set out all the things in some pretty fashion, so we left them in charge while we gave Willie a hand with the rabbits. He spends so much time taking them in and out of the cages that he would never get them set up on display in time for judging without our help. I've heard that last summer Willie took mangoes to German school to rile the other students. He teases them by tossing the mangoes into the air, and the other students cause a ruckus by scrambling around for them. I've told Rev. Thieme to use a firm hand with that boy; we sure do at home.

I wish you had been with us at the Fair. There were so many things on display that I can't begin to list all the categories. Only in America would people enter their babies in "The Baby Show" to be judged as "The Cutest" or "The Fattest"! And, Pauline, you would have loved the Fancy Work division with all the embroidery, needlepoint, and lace work. They even had a category for antiques and curios. Our friend, John Zill, drew a prize for having the oldest Bible,

Willie and Clara play with the rabbits that Willie raised as his responsibility.

nearly two hundred years old. But Pastor Thieme won the first prize for the oldest book in Palm Beach County, a book that was three hundred and sixty-seven years old.

We checked on Willie, and sure enough, he was running around over by his exhibit, trying to find one of the rabbits he let get away, and not too happy to see Papa coming. Clara and Annie had the vegetable display set up, and we were pleased to see all the work and imagination they'd put into it. They couldn't have been prouder when the Flagler prize of $100 went to "A. Hofman for the Best General Exhibit in the

Willie, Clara, and Annie stand in the Hofman pineapple fields, which stretched all the way from Northeast Seventh Avenue to Swinton Avenue in 1913.

Vegetable Department." They were especially excited to see that ribbon for all their efforts, and I'm sure they were more than proud that we let them do it alone.

We spent the rest of the afternoon walking around the displays, talking to our friends and catching up on all the news. Sadie Sundy won a special prize for the best chocolate cake, and well she deserves it. Her cakes are delicious. Over at the curio display, we saw that Mrs. Thieme had won for the best specimen of hand-painted china. Willie found his missing rabbit, and even though he didn't get a prize, I think he was happy just to put them on display, not to mention the piece of chocolate cake Sadie gave him.

I so wish you could have been with us, dear sister. Give my greetings to all the relatives over there.

> My love to all the family,
> Anna

Delray, June 23, 1914

Dear Pauline,

 I went to make a pot of hasenpfeffer the other afternoon and found out I needed more vinegar. For wine I had to make do with some of Adolf's pineapple wine he makes in the packing house. The out-of-town visitors are wild about it and always manage to buy some when they stop for citrus and other fruit. I figure it ought to taste good in that rabbit stew, but I still needed the vinegar. Willie was nowhere around and Clara was at the German school, so that left Annie to go to the store for me.
 Did I ever tell you Annie has quite an independent streak in her just like Adolf? She can be just as strong-willed and headstrong as he is once her mind is made up. Well, when I asked her, she got it into her mind to take the automobile over to the store, saying it was too hot to ride the bicycle. The only problem was that she never once drove a car alone, even though she's been after Adolf to teach her how. Good thing he was way off in the fields, since the next thing I saw was Annie sitting up in the driver's seat determined to take off for town. I watched her through the kitchen window because I knew there was no stopping her once she got a notion inside her head. She even called Mr. Etter from the fields to crank the car for her, which he did, reluctantly.
 Well, he got the car started all right, and Annie began fiddling around with the gearshift and clutch. There was a lot of scraping and whining, and the car was jerking forward a few inches every now and

Annie enjoys the Florida sun and foliage. Her favorite flowers were roses and carnations, which she kept planted around the Hofman home.

then. The longer it took, the more determined Annie got that she was going to get that car out of the driveway. She must have found the right gear from watching Adolf do it often enough because, suddenly, she shot forward off the grass and onto the rock driveway and around the circle. Around she went, the car lurching and bouncing, sitting up tall in the seat, hanging on to the steering wheel. Away she went, and that was the last I saw of her for some time.

Willie came home with the mail from the post office and a bottle of vinegar.

"How did you get that?" I asked.

"Oh, Annie told me you needed it."

"Well, that was hours ago, where is she?"

"She's sitting over in town on the car's running board mad as can be. She couldn't get the gears in reverse, and half the men in town were trying to tell her how when she accidentally found the right gear and yanked the car in reverse. It shot back clear across the street and hit the sharp curbstones in front of the sidewalk. She popped the two back tires with everybody around watching. Mr. Burton helped me put on the spare, but she's still sitting there with one flat tire."

"Wait till Papa hears about this," I answered.

Willie found Adolf in the fields, and Adolf took off for town to bring back Annie and buy another tire for the rear axle. At the time, he sure was not happy, but later I think he secretly admired Annie for her gumption. She hasn't gone near the car since, but knowing her, she's headed for town again before long. The hasenpfeffer tasted good.

> My love to all of you,
> Anna

Adolf and Anna proudly display the family car. Over the years, they owned various automobiles, which included a Model T Ford, an Overland, a Jewett, an Oldsmobile, and a Nash.

Clara, Adolf and Anna's second daughter, was the first of the Hofman family to leave Delray and to try a career other than working on the family farm. Her letter of December 26, 1918 also mentions her cousin in Germany, Paul A. Dreher, who, years later, contributed to the development of West Palm Beach.

Clara said she was tired of milking the family cow named Betsy and longed to get away to the city of Miami.

Delray, December 26, 1918

Dear Uncle Paul,

    I'm home for Christmas after living in Miami for almost a year. Mama and Papa have friends there who promised to watch over me while I am living at the Miami YWCA. I enrolled in a business school in Miami, and I am taking courses in bookkeeping. What I really want to do is stay there and work as a bookkeeper. I've had enough of milking cows on the farm.

    Mama asked me to write and tell you that Papa said it would be fine to have cousin Paul [Paul Albert Dreher, Jr.] come to America in a few years to stay with us. Papa certainly needs full-time help on the farm, and Paul can work off his passage money and living expenses by working on the property as agreed. Annie and Willie are looking forward to having someone to talk with now that I am gone to Miami. Sometimes the farm chores get tedious, and it is always the same routine day after day. Delray is so small and there's not much news to talk about.

    I hope Paul will take care of the chickens just as lovingly as I did since I still think of them as my pets, and I don't want them ignored now that I'm gone. It always broke my heart when Papa or Mama killed one for our dinner. Whenever I thought of one of my own pets being killed, I could never eat chicken at home.

    When Paul comes here to work on the farm, Papa plans to convert a small section of the packing house for Paul's bedroom. I know that Paul will think it's an adventure to be out there on his own with the sweet smell of mangoes ripening on the other side of the packing house wall as they wait to be packed and shipped. I know he'll love the taste of those delicious blueberries, or huckleberries, growing wild down by the canal. I like to walk to the canal and pick those berries and eat them right out of my hand. They're my favorite food.

The best thing happened to me at the end of my last year of school in Delray. My teacher coaxed me into entering the Palm Beach County baking contest. With her coaching me, I actually won. As a result, I went to the college in Tallahassee for a two-week course in home economics. I really enjoyed the experience of getting away from home on my own and meeting new people.

Papa bought a piano a few years ago and said that I was the one who had to learn to play it since Annie plays in the church band and Willie plays the trombone in the community band. Papa says I might have to play the organ at church some day, so I needed to learn how to read music. I spent several years learning to play the piano whether I wanted to or not. Papa had his mind set on it.

Please say hello to Aunt Mathilde, Aunt Pauline, and the rest of the relatives. Mama and Papa also send their love and greetings to all of you.

Love from your niece,
Clara

Paul A. Dreher ∞ Dreher Park

As Clara had hoped, her cousin did come to live in Delray. Paul Dreher, one of Anna's nephews in Erpfingen, emigrated from Germany in 1924 with fifty dollars he had borrowed from the Hofmans. Paul had already earned a degree in horticulture in Germany.

While living with the Hofmans and working for Adolf, Dreher learned about propagating tropical plants and trees. Even though Paul was Anna's nephew, Adolf was a stern and exacting employer. Paul slept in a room built for him in Adolf's packing house and was required to work long, demanding hours.

Some years later, he left Delray and went to West Palm Beach where he worked for the public parks from 1931 to 1962. He was the driving force behind filling marshes and building Currie, Phipps, and Howard parks. Eventually, he was named the city's first Director of Parks. He got the Lake Worth Drainage District to drain an area west of West Palm Beach, and with almost no municipal funding, moved the city's nursery there. He then began to stock the park with trees, plants, and shrubs. Dreher also added a number of small animals to the park. The park was named in honor of Dreher in 1957 and continued to grow. In 1997 the park was renamed Palm Beach Zoo at Dreher Park.

Delray outdoorsmen line up for an outing on the frontier west of town. Hunting in the Everglades was a favorite pastime and diversion from daily chores.

While Clara attended business school in Miami, William attended high school in Delray and enjoyed his own adventures in the surrounding area.

Delray, November 29, 1919

Dear Uncle Paul,

Let me tell you about my trip to the Everglades to hunt wild turkey for Thanksgiving. Mama always wants a fresh turkey since we get tired of quail and chicken around here. Papa said I was old enough to take the .22 rifle to the Glades only if I went with a group of men. So he arranged for me to go with John Lamb, who was heading out that way with some friends. He knows more about the wetlands area than anyone else around here.

We headed west of town to Military Trail. Then we pushed farther north, northwest, to the Loxahatchee wetlands area west of Jupiter where we borrowed a narrow skiff and two canoes from Mr. Lamb's friend. It was a regular Glades boat, a shallow, flat-bottomed skiff, about sixteen feet long, made with a wedge-shaped bow to cut through the water.

We put in at a small stream flowing east, and in short time, we were swallowed up in tall trees and swamps. Mr. Lamb knew how to read the flow, so we drifted slowly along between the tree trunks with shallow stretches of water on all sides of us. Ospreys and herons were everywhere. Small turtles stretching for some sunlight darted into the water as we approached.

Young gators clung to the banks, their eyes bobbing open and shut as we glided past them. We knew the mother gators would be close by. My rifle was right beside me, and several men toted their shotguns in the canoes. There was a large gator track along one bank, a long, wet streak through the sand. We came upon several alligator holes where the waters deepened along the shoreline into small open ponds. The gators tunnel in and lie hidden for hours without coming to the surface for air. But gators were not what we were after this time.

More than once, we veered off into a dead-end fork whenever the shallow water broadened out wider and wider. We also had to portage the skiff and canoes across sand bars and fallen tree trunks barring our way. John scooped up handfuls of water and sand from the riverbed. He scraped through the sand of what was once an old ocean bed. Sure enough, he found shark teeth, which he tossed into his knapsack to add to his collection back home. I took some, too. Late that afternoon, we pitched our tents on a grassy hummock, had supper, and settled down for the night. In the darkness, raccoons circled our camp, their eyes glowing from the firelight, hungry for food.

The next morning we were on the river again. After paddling for some time, we let the boats drift, sat motionless, and looked for turkey in the grasslands just beyond the trees. Even though we could not find any there, we knew we would find several turkeys gathered in the dense trees of the hummocks. We spotted a covey, and I began calling, or "keouking," trying to get the turkeys to come into range. It took some time, but sure enough, it worked. Then I took my .22 and drew a bead on the turkey. I slowly

William enjoyed skinning raccoons and stretching their skins, which tourists eagerly purchased.

cocked the rifle and pulled the trigger. We bagged four birds right there at one time and continued till we came across more wild turkeys. Got them, too.

Loaded with fowl, we began the long trip back, using all our strength as we paddled against the current this time. There were many logs and sand bars to portage again, but our bounty and the thoughts of a big turkey meal kept us going. Near the end of the trip, right off shore, I raised the rifle and shot three raccoons to use for the skins. Mama hates to have the skins around stretched out and nailed on a board drying in the sun, but tourists in town still pay good money for a full skin, and it's no problem for me. I'm used to skinning squirrels whenever I shoot them out of the mango trees 'cause they bring money too, and Papa doesn't want those squirrels eating all the fruit.

  We returned the skiff and canoes and headed for home. Mama and the girls sure had their work cut out for them getting those turkeys fixed for Thanksgiving. You and Paul, Jr. should think about coming over here to visit us so we can take you to the Glades on a hunting trip.

Your godson,
Willie

From Farmland to Land Development
The Florida Boom

The passing years brought significant changes to the economy of Delray Beach. As a result of drainage operations in the Lake Worth Drainage District, the water table had been lowered, depriving the pineapples of the moisture needed to grow to full size. Moreover, planting pineapples in the same fields year after year robbed the soil of nutrients. Competition from the Cuban pineapple market, fostered by Flagler's overseas railway to Key West, caused the Delray growers to lose money. With the diminished pineapple market and the demise of the Delray canning factory, Adolf began to view land more and more as a commodity to be developed and sold for real estate purposes. As far back as 1912, he had experimented with land promotion and listed some of his land for sale in the Delray Improvement Association.

As the population grew and the demand for neighborhoods increased in Delray, Hofman played a role in this trend by developing several notable tracts. First, he platted the neighborhood surrounding his own house in 1913 and named it the Hofman Addition. This was the section from Northeast Seventh Avenue to the railroad tracks between Northeast Fifth Street and Northeast Seventh Street. Its variety of citrus trees and other tropical fruit trees planted on the property as a part of Adolf's own estate beautified the lots and welcomed property buyers.

By the early 1920s, the great Florida Land Boom was under way, and its giddy effects were felt in Delray. Sales agents flocked to the charming town with its empty acres ripe for promotion and development. Many of the land

Adolf examines some of his citrus fruit in 1916.

sale promotions sported real estate agents in dapper knickers accompanied by uniformed bands playing music to help hawk land sales. Spirits soared. Prices rose dramatically, and land speculation became the sport of the season.

Once again, the Florida East Coast freight trains rode the rails, carrying both a blessing and a curse during the building boom of the 1920s. Lumber and construction materials arrived by rail daily, fueling the building frenzy precipitated by land speculators and grossly inflated property prices. During this exciting period in Delray, Hofman was actively promoting his own land for sale, as evidenced in the platting of several new neighborhoods.

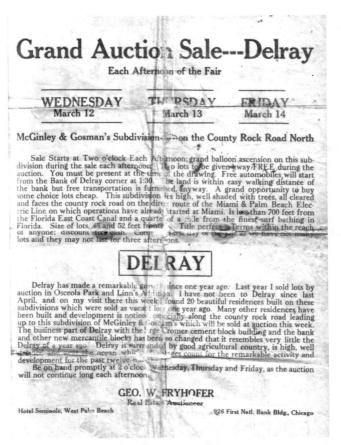

This 1913 flier promoted an early Delray land sale for the McKinley & Gosman subdivision, east of the railroad tracks, north of the Hofman homestead.

Adolf and Anna owned one third of the land that now comprises the Del-Ida Park neighborhood. They sold the property in 1923 to promote the development of Del-Ida Park. It was the first planned residential development in Delray, and its Mediterranean Revival and Mission Style residences contributed a quaint charm to the neighborhood.

In 1924, together with the Hall family and L.E. Perkins, Adolf platted the area known as Las Palmas, located just to the west of the canal, between Fourth Street and Fifth Street. The Las Palmas development was originally envisioned to be a luxurious neighborhood of gracious Mediterranean Revival homes. Instead, it became a modest and quiet neighborhood near the canal.

Clara, Annie, Anna, and Adolf stand in front of one of the family automobiles.

Delray, September 30, 1923

My Dear Sister,

My love and greetings to all of you. It was good to hear that your family is getting along fine.

Adolf and I had a full day today driving around Delray and talking to our lawyer, Mr. C.Y. Byrd, about our future plans. What a close and loyal friend he has been through the years. Now that he's planning to move his practice from West Palm Beach to Delray, it will be easier to have him handle our legal matters. He agrees with Adolf that the times are ripe for selling some of our pineapple fields for property.

Along with most of South Florida, Delray is caught up in the land fever, or Boom, as it is known. With more and more tourists coming south to Florida, farmland is now worth much more money as real estate for new houses and neighborhoods. Hosts of land speculators have flocked into town. Advertisements promoting land sales are placed in prominent northern newspapers, and handbills are distributed all over town. Prices are soaring and land is being bought and sold at phenomenal prices.

Mr. Byrd has cautioned us not to believe all the rumors, for many of the transactions take place only by verbal agreement or with a small binder. He wants Adolf to make sure he has a firm commitment in writing from a reputable buyer and a sizeable binder to hold the contract.

So the three of us took the car west of the railroad tracks to the old acreage Adolf bought in 1896 where he planted pineapple fields stretching all the way to Swinton Avenue. Mr. Byrd heard that a new corporation, the Ocean City Development Company, is planning to develop a huge tract of land around that area. The company was eager to purchase our acres since their development will extend both north and south of our land. Adolf thought it was time to risk something new with the land, and heaven knows we got our use out of that land from all the years of planting and harvesting.

Later in the afternoon, the three of us met with the officers of the Ocean City Development Company. They led us into their offices where all of us looked over the plat proposed for their development. The new area would be a neighborhood named Del-Ida Park and would include many houses built in a type of Spanish style, or Mediterranean Revival style as they called it. Some of the streets were laid out in a diagonal pattern, creating little courts or islands of property.

I was intrigued with the idea that old farmland could be turned into something as attractive as this. Since about one-third of the land they needed for Del-Ida Park belonged to us, they negotiated with Adolf and Check Byrd for some time and finally made us a formal offer at an acceptable price. After consulting with Mr. Byrd, we agreed to the purchase price and went ahead and signed the papers. We felt confident that he would finalize all the necessary papers.

It gives me a strange feeling to see our old land pass from our hands, but the days of raising pineapples are over, and with the new demand for land, we are wise to try something different. Years ago, way back in 1913, even before the land boom started, Adolf tried his hand at turning our land into real estate. He hired surveyors to plat the area around our home into lots for sale. It has met with some success so far.

As you can see, our world is changing here in Delray. We are no longer the village by the canal. Now we are called the "City of Destiny." It was impossible to even think of such a claim when we first eked out our living on the partially cleared land. Those days brought us so many backaches and hardships. Yes, we loved that land because it was ours and we belonged to it.

Man thinks he changes the landscape, but instead, the landscape changes him as it becomes a part of him. And the land will outlast all of us and endure forever. Still, it's sad to see the land change and lose its old identity. The whippoorwills no longer call at twilight, and the blue heron no longer lifts her wings.

> Best wishes and love,
> Anna

William sits on the steps of the Delray High School in his senior year, 1923.

Delray, October 28, 1924

Dear Uncle Gustav,

I wanted to write you to let you know that since my high graduation last year, I have been attending Twentieth Century Business College in West Palm Beach. I am also working as a bookkeeper and teller in the Delray Bank and Trust Co. Just think, it's been almost twenty years since you came to America for my baptism.

Let me tell you what is happening with me in Delray. I am still playing in the city marching band organized by Mr. Al Miller. He has also been my music teacher for several years. Last year, Papa bought me a silver trombone made by J.W. York and Sons from Grand Rapids, Michigan, and I've been taking music lessons ever since. Because I play the trombone, I have to march in the very front row of the band, following Mr. Miller. Believe me, it's not easy to march, read the music clipped onto the instrument, and maneuver the sliding trombone arm all at the same time. The pastor of our church, Rev. Rudolph Keyl, is also in Mr. Miller's band and plays the bass tuba. We usually play for the Fourth of July parades, the county fairs, and for any other special occasion in town. I also play my trombone in the band for the land sales that are going on all over town right now. We have to wear a uniform with a dark blazer, white pants, and a white helmet hat to impress tourists and prospective land buyers.

Last year, I played on the Delray High School basketball team. Every day, we practiced after school on the outside court on the schoolhouse square. We won a lot of games, but we had to travel far away to play other teams, which made it even more fun.

Even though I was a senior in high school last year, I was in the same classroom of the Delray School that I had in other years. It was the southwest corner room upstairs, where I could look out over the school square and the main street of town when I got tired of listening to the teacher at the blackboard. There were only three students in my senior class, Elizabeth Scott, Paul Dean, and myself. I was the third smartest in my class. My favorite subject was mathematics, which is simple for me. I am now attending the business school in West Palm Beach, planning to be an accountant or a banker one day. After all the years I worked growing up on the farm, I'm not interested in being a farmer. Mama always said over and over again, "Don't ever be a farmer!"

Besides, Papa is gradually selling off his farmland as lots for houses. There is a great deal of buying and selling in Delray now that so many tourists visit during the winter and even settle here. There may not even be many farms left around town in the future. In America things change fast, and Delray is growing fast, too.

I hope that all is well with you and the other relatives in Monchhof. Papa sends his greetings also.

Your godson,
Willie

The Delray High School basketball team enjoyed a good season in 1922. Front row, left to right: Lamar Barwick, Theron Mervin, Willard Waters. Back row, left to right: Walter Godbold, William Hofman

Late in 1925, the Florida East Coast Railway could not meet the increasing demand for shipping building supplies and declared an embargo on shipments to southeast Florida. Building ceased and land sales plummeted. The embargo edict of the iron titan wiped out potential real estate profits for Adolf. Once again, the railway that cut through Hofman's land pandering transport and profit also cut through his attempts at financial advancement.

ADOLF HOFMAN
Grower of
FANCY FRUITS AND VEGETABLES
Delray -- Florida

January 18, 1925

Dear Brother Fritz and family,

I received your letter and I am glad you are well, which I can also say of my family. My second daughter is still employed in Miami as a bookkeeper, while my eldest is still at home with us and has to help her mother. My son is employed here at the bank as a bookkeeper, since farming has paid off so miserably during the last four years that he was in no mood to become a farmer. Therefore, I sent him to a business school in West Palm Beach.

At most, I plant one fourth as many vegetables as I did ten years ago. My main business is pineapples, which have still yielded quite good profit even though

Cuba still ships three to four million crates of them to the United States. Furthermore, I have bananas, oranges, and grapefruit that I can sell for the most part directly to tourists. As many as ten to fifteen cars call every day, so I have gained in time good customers, and the old customers bring new customers. In this way, I get to know people from all the States and keep them as my customers.

Since Delray is growing and the lots fetch colossal prices, I will divide my land between the canal and railroad into lots. I sold my land west of the railroad two years ago. The company that bought it has subdivided it [today's Del-Ida Park neighborhood] and has built roads, and now it's all sold. The northern capitalists are just crazy about buying land on the southern east coast, and the price has risen at least tenfold in the last two years. Many farmers sold their land some years ago, when prices for produce were so low, for a very cheap price. And now, if they had only held out, they could be rich people.

With my nephew Paul and with Mr. Etter, I am not quite satisfied so far. As to my nephew, I think that in time I can break him in quite well, but I expect not to have much use for Etter, for he is too sentimentally disposed. Such a man should not emigrate. He will never be suited for farming here since he cannot work independently and also takes no interest in nature.

I still don't know if I can come to Germany this year. I had thought that I would have broken in one of those fellows sufficiently to substitute for me, but there can be no thought of this. For my Negroes don't have the least respect for them. They take orders from the Negroes. I cannot leave now because there is so much work that needs to be done in my packing house. I might be able to leave in August or September, but my wife has no desire to go. She became far too seasick on the passage from Germany when she first came here years ago. She vows never to board a ship again.

When I sent you the food draft [a type of economic assistance after WW I] I never expected that you would reimburse me. I ask you that you under no circumstances send me any money. If you should absolutely want to get rid of it, then please give it to a poor family in real need. If you know some families who suffer bitter need, send me their addresses so that we can send them something.

I could sell my land now for a very high price, even though rumors have it that the railway can't keep up with the supply and demand for building materials. Perhaps it is best to sell before the railway stops transporting lumber. The realtors keep pestering me, but I don't want to sell because I would have to give the government too much for income tax. Thus, I will only sell five to ten building lots per year. That way my income taxes are not too high, and my remaining land will still gain in value.

Many greetings,
Adolf

Adolf loved to wander around his property tending to his crops, which included these banana trees he cultivated.

Adolf built his own packing house where he packed and shipped crates of pineapples, mangoes, and other tropical fruits.

The Arcade Building

In its heyday the Arcade Building was one of the most beautiful buildings ever to grace downtown Delray. At one time, its imposing façade, embellished with trellises of bougainvillea, towered over Atlantic Avenue and commanded attention. The Mediterranean Revival architecture, designed by Delray architect Samuel Ogren, Sr., featured barrel-tiled octagonal turrets on the second story above the entrance portal. The Hofman family played an important role in the history of the building for over five decades.

Adolf purchased the site of the Arcade Building, Lots 2 and 3 of Block 100, from L.G. Lyman and his wife

Delray architect Samuel Ogren, Sr. drew this architectural rendering of the Arcade Building, which was constructed in 1925. (Courtesy of Delray Beach Historical Society)

Kate Lyman on January 26, 1907. This was one of Adolf's early real estate ventures. On April 30, 1925, Adolf and Anna leased the property to the Atlantic Avenue Company with the stipulation that a building be erected on the site within one year. The large and impressive building was completed, but apparently the company had financial trouble. Matters grew worse, and since the Atlantic Avenue Company could not live up to the lease and meet the mortgage payments, Adolf had to file the notice of foreclosure on September 14, 1927. As a result, Adolf and Anna now regained control of the property and acquired the Arcade Building unexpectedly.

The building sat partially vacant for some time while Hofman, who did not really want the building at first, decided the best way to utilize it. In time, he rented out more and more space for offices and shops, and the arrangement proved quite successful. In 1931 the famous cartoonist, Fontaine Fox, creator of the cartoon "Toonerville Trolley," rented an office, which he used as his studio, on the second floor of the Arcade Building. H.T. Webster, creator of "Casper Milquetoast — The Timid Soul," also had an office upstairs. Soon other artists rented office or studio space, and for years the building was filled with lively and creative personalities. The Arcade Building became home to a growing colony of artists and writers.

Local residents also rented space for their businesses. Al Miller, who organized the first Boy Scout troop and formed the community marching band, had a barbershop on the right side of the Arcade entrance. Sadie Sundy's Beauty Shop and Adams' Florist occupied street-front shops, and other downstairs tenants included realtor Matt Gracy and land developer Clint Moore. The Hofmans continued to rent out the arcade shops and office spaces for the next several decades.

The famous Arcade Tap Room was established in 1933 by the personable Bill Kraus. Under his legendary management, it grew from a sandwich shop into a prestigious place to dine. It became a popular mecca for authors, socialites, and celebrities in the 1930s and 1940s. Among them were writers Hugh McNair Kahler, Clarence B. Kelland, Nina Wilcox Putnam, and poet

The Arcade Tap Room was the social center of Delray's cultural life for several decades. (Courtesy of Delray Beach Historical Society)

Edna St. Vincent Millay. As part of the artists' and writers' colony, they gathered in the Tap Room in the late afternoons for stimulating conversation over dinner and drinks. Joining them were illustrators such as

Charles Williams and Herb Niblick. The walls were lined with book jackets, cartoons, sketches, and paintings. In addition, a growing winter colony of socialites, golfers, polo players, and political figures also frequented the Tap Room.

Bill Kraus continued to popularize the open-air courtyard as a chic dining area where tall palm trees swayed gently beneath the moon and stars. Its lovely patio, featuring a terraced fountain in the center, became increasingly fashionable under his management. Dining out at the stylish Arcade Tap Room was an elegant and festive occasion. There was warmth and conviviality those days in Delray when celebrities and local merchants mingled in the Tap Room and felt at home together.

The Tap Room remained the social hub of Delray for several decades, but the ensuing years brought changes to its décor and atmosphere. Under new management in the fifties, the dining area was remodeled, and a glass roof was installed over the patio. The remodeled area lost much of the charm and ambiance it purveyed when polo players and celebrities frequented the original Tap Room. In the sixties another new manager struggled to revitalize the Arcade dining room once again. In 1970 the Hofman family leased the building to Arcade Reality, Inc. The Hofman family continued to own the Arcade Building until they finally sold it to Arcade Realty, Inc. on January 3, 1978.

Delray Beach, August 3, 1927

My Dear Sister Pauline,

As always, I have more news to share with you about the changing times in Delray. Just this year, the name of our little town has been changed again. Too bad our dear Mama is not still alive, as she would recall when our area was first known as Zion, then as Linton, and then as Delray. Now, the Town of Delray and the area east of the canal known as the Town of Delray Beach have officially merged, and together we are now known as the City of Delray Beach.

We had to drive to our lawyer's office to sign some legal documents today. Annie does the driving, thank goodness, now that there are more and more cars in town. Adolf insisted that I come along since my name now appears on the official documents. With advice from Check Byrd, our attorney, Adolf incorporated our names for legal reasons. We even have an official seal to emboss our legal papers. Never did I ever imagine I would become incorporated, but that's the way of things nowadays.

Adolf wants to develop more of our land as real estate. Mr. Byrd advised Adolf to work only with a trustworthy realtor. At the height of the land Boom, too many unscrupulous real estate agents, or boomers, not even from Delray, promoted and boasted about land sales at outrageous prices. Now that the prices have peaked and fallen and the boomers have left town, it's time for Adolf to make his move.

Adolf has had some luck with real estate already. He showed good judgment twenty years ago in 1907 when he bought some lots from the Lymans right downtown on the main street. Just two years ago, the Arcade Building was constructed on those lots we leased, and by default we acquired ownership of the building.

What a lovely structure it is, broad and stately, with two small octagonal cupolas on top of the second story. Enormous vines of purple bougainvillea cling to the outer walls and create an arch over the entry. Just inside the main entrance, thick cypress beams with carved moldings support the decorative ceiling. A broad, arched passageway leads to the patio. Inside, there are small shops clustered around the arcade, which is open to the air so that people can stroll around from shop to shop and enjoy the sunshine. The shops seem busy with people coming and going, and thus we have some steady income every month.

Adolf said that now is the time to plat more of our land so developers and realtors will promote it. We met our friend Matt Gracey, the finest real estate agent in Delray, and the most honorable, and asked him to join us as we went to look over our land on the east side of the canal. So off we went, with Annie driving and Matt Gracey along with us, bouncing over the wood plank drawbridge, to look at all that old muck land property east of the canal, north of Atlantic Avenue.

I cannot believe that anyone could ever think of living in that mosquito-ridden, low-lying area. When I think of all the years Adolf and his old mule spent plowing that land, it breaks my heart. We did get our share of tomatoes, beans, and peppers over the years, though. But Adolf said we have to build for the future because Delray will not always be a farming town. Even though the Land Boom is over, he thinks that the future of land development for serious investors is still ahead of us. When I see how much farming has aged him over the years, I know it is time to look ahead.

When the men had finished looking around, Annie insisted we drive farther on, east to the beach road, then a little north, to see the ruins of the old Orange Grove House of Refuge that burned down in March of this year. I dreaded the thought of seeing such sadness.

The Orange Grove House of Refuge appeared alone and abandoned shortly before it burned to the ground in 1927.

How my heart ached when I saw the spot vacant and charred. The only remnants left of Zion were scorched timbers and blackened roof beams lying in the ashes. I could not bear to look for long. All I wanted to remember was Annie Andrews running to greet me and welcome me to Zion years ago when I first arrived here as a stranger in an alien land. Even after the Andrews left, I thought of the house not only as a place of refuge, but also as a sacred fortress that would stand forever. Now it is gone. How the years have claimed us all.

Home to our house with supper to make, my heart was full of conflicting emotions about the past and about the future. I am filled with sorrow that the past has vanished, yet I am also filled with hope that the land, as always, will lift our hearts and sustain us in the future.

Your loving sister,
Anna

Hofman's Development of Delray Beach Neighborhoods

Adolf developed several new neighborhoods in Delray Beach as he gradually turned more and more farmland into real estate. As noted earlier, he had already platted the Hofman Addition in 1913, sold land to promote Del-Ida Park in 1923, and shared in platting Las Palmas in 1924. All three plats were residential neighborhoods that helped to expand Delray Beach. As their real estate ventures grew, Adolf and Anna incorporated their holdings and became Hofman and Hofman, Inc. in 1927. Their daughter Annie served as secretary of the small corporation.

Adolf platted part of his original sixty acres on the west bank of the canal in 1936 and named it Hofman Village. The plat was divided into three large blocks between Fifth Street and Seventh Street. This old farmland evolved into a picturesque neighborhood with its own distinctive atmosphere. The charming and quiet neighborhood was known for its winding trail, rustling cabbage palms, and meandering Hofman Lane. Lush tropical vegetation threaded its way through Hofman Village and continued to the canal. Today the area is known as the Palm Trail neighborhood.

With road contractor and developer Clint Moore and realtor Matt Gracey, Hofman platted and developed the section known as Ocean Breeze Estates, east of the canal, in 1937. This is the lovely area surrounding Seabreeze Avenue. This fashionable neighborhood within walking distance of the ocean is still known for its beautiful and impressive rows of stately Royal Palm trees planted by Adolf in 1937.

Adolf stands on Seabreeze Avenue in 1937, the main street in his Ocean Breeze Estates subdivision. Adolf had the street lined with graceful Royal Palm trees. Note the lone house on the right.

Hofman's stately Royal Palm trees still grace Seabreeze Avenue in 2004. Note that the same house remains, located on the right.

On the moist, fertile soil east of the canal, where he once planted part of his vegetable crop, Hofman, along with Matt Gracey, began developing Waterway Lane in 1940. This secluded lane leading to the canal ended in an elegant cul-de-sac. The Ocean Breeze Estates development and the Waterway Lane projects greatly benefited Delray Beach by filling in the low, marshy land that had been a perennial breeding place for mosquitoes.

Two more neighborhood developments grew out of Adolf's original sixty acres. Martha and Hal Hall purchased Block Number 3 of the Hofman Village section and platted it as Martha's Vineyard in 1947. Adolf's last major land development in Delray Beach, platted as Hofman's Eighth Avenue Addition, came in 1950 and ran between Northeast Fifth Street and Northeast Seventh Street, opposite Martha's Vineyard and Hofman Village. A luxuriant umbrella of mango trees shaded the avenue and invited residents seeking a quiet, tranquil neighborhood.

Adolf in later years continued to enjoy his mango trees and other groves he had carefully tended throughout his life.

The 1928 Hurricane

On September 16, 1928, one of the deadliest hurricanes ever to hit South Florida tore through Delray Beach and brought even greater damage and death to the Lake Okeechobee area. The torrential rain was recorded at ten inches in that area. Winds estimated at 145 miles per hour blew huge quantities of water out of Lake Okeechobee, which was already at high level from heavy summer rains. A wall of water ten feet high hit Pahokee, Belle Glade, and South Bay, killing thousands of residents.

The savage hurricane battered Delray Beach Sunday afternoon, September 16, and continued all through the night. The center of the hurricane passed over the town

Trinity Evangelical Lutheran Church suffered great damage from being blown sideways and was actually blown off its foundation by the fury of the 1928 hurricane. (Courtesy of Trinity Lutheran Church Archives)

with winds estimated at 125 miles per hour. During the fury of the storm, the winds blew in from the northeast and tilted the wooden sanctuary of Trinity Lutheran Church to the southwest. After the eye of the hurricane had passed, the direction of the winds reversed, and the small church was tilted in the opposite direction and blown off its foundation. The Atlantic Store and other downtown stores were leveled. In Del Ida Park the hurricane blew the roof off a house and hurled it onto a neighbor's garage. Porches were torn off houses and several chimneys caved in.

The *Delray Beach News* reported that 227 houses were destroyed and 350 families were homeless as a result of raging winds and heavy rainfall. Sources confirmed that only three people in Delray Beach died as a result of the storm. Although Delray Beach suffered intense property damage, the Hofman home, along with other structures in town, survived the storm.

Delray Beach, September 18, 1928

Dear Brother Fritz and Family,

Your newspapers have no doubt carried the news of the terrible storm that hit our area. Here in Delray, the violent hurricane struck full force. Thank God we are well but have suffered great property damage. Many houses and trees in Delray Beach have been destroyed by this massive hurricane, the worst yet ever to hit our part of Florida. Everywhere, the streets are filled with rubble and standing water, which has nowhere to drain since the soil is thoroughly saturated from the torrential rains.

We first got the news of the approaching storm on Sunday morning. It seemed impossible since the sky was bright and clear that morning. Still we took warning and cancelled the church service. Even at noon the sky was bright, but around two o'clock in the afternoon, the winds began to blow, and we could tell the storm was coming in fast. When it finally hit us full force, we had by then stored sufficient water from our water tower and pumped fresh water for cooking and drinking just in case the water supply should fail.

As the storm raged, we huddled downstairs in the middle of the house, with the lights off, and prayed to God for the best. We could see that the house was leaning from the force of the gales, and we could feel the house shake a number of times. The noise outside was deafening. From the sound of things, we knew trees were cracking everywhere around us. Several windows in the attic and upstairs bedrooms were broken by coconuts and palm fronds tossed about by the force of the winds. The heavy winds and rains continued to lash the house.

During the eye of the storm, we went outside only to find the barn blown down and lying in complete ruins on its stone foundation. At least we no longer had the cows and horse, for they, too, would have perished in all that rubble. Also, from where we could see, the car looked quite damaged, wedged underneath the ruins of the barn.

After the eye of the storm passed over us, the winds hit with a fury from the opposite direction. We hurried back into the house to wait out the rest of the storm, and sure enough, the house leaned and shook again from the opposite direction and all the windows rattled. Gales of wind drove the rain sideways through cracks around the doors and window jams. So began the long task of mopping up. We could hear the coconut palms thrashing against the sides of the house upstairs, and we were sure more windows were going to break.

When finally it was over the next day, we counted up our losses. Huge limbs from some twelve to twenty mango trees were ripped from the trees, and eight or nine coconut palms were either blown down or snapped off at the top. Litter and rubble were strewn everywhere. As I said, the barn was down, and shingles from our house roof were scattered everywhere. We are thankful the house was saved and none of us were injured.

In town, Schrader's chimney was blown away, and some downtown buildings were totally destroyed. Eggers' house was completely knocked down, and he suffered a broken leg and has been hospitalized. Our church was blown sideways. Although tilted at a dangerous angle, it still stands. Much other damage did the church suffer and barely survived the storm, which battered it unmercifully. Some claim that the winds were as high as 130 to 140 miles per hour, but who can say for sure? Again, we thank God that we were spared from this calamity, the worst catastrophe ever to hit Delray.

Your brother,
Adolf

Adolf and Anna continued to write letters to their relatives in Germany over the years. The selection of letters in this book, however, concludes with Anna's letter of December 28, 1928.

Delray Beach, December 28, 1928

Dear Pauline,

I thought I would rest a bit from my needlepoint since my eyes are strained from the close work. I still have my needlepoint materials out because the Ladies' Aid Society at Trinity was making new altar cloths for the church now that the hurricane damage is being repaired. Several weeks ago, I got out my thread and needles, and we took turns sewing at each other's houses. We worked on new altar cloths and communion linens for the liturgical seasons of the church year. Our wooden church was blown off its foundation by the recent hurricane and was leaning far to one side. That old church has seen some wear over the years, but I'm glad we can repair it and hold on to a little of the past.

Maybe I'm thinking so much about the past today because it was thirty-three years ago today that I arrived in Zion on the canal barge, not knowing the language and having only Adolf there for family and friend. It reminds me of the old times and the hard times we had of it, clearing the land and getting the crops put in. We had no roads or town to speak of at first, just lonely miles of sand and palmettos.

It reminds me of what Sophie Frey told me she did whenever she got tired. She would close her eyes and picture in her mind how the land looked years ago, and that brought her peace. She could still see the sand trails and the few shell roads we had as her mind traced the stores and houses in Delray from years back, remembering the old settlers and wondering what had become of them all. We had strong souls in those days. We fought the frontier and cleared the land and thought little of it, as if it were our destiny to conquer this ragged edge of the continent.

Sophie wrote it all down in her journal. "In midsummer I cleared two acres of farmland with my own hands, dug my own ditches, put in the seed, and harvested my crop. Life was hard but living was cheap. We had fresh vegetables and on Sundays chicken, rabbit, or fish. For two seasons I rented land in the flatwoods where there were no houses and no undergrowth, only some tall pine trees. You could hear the owls and alligators and sometimes a wildcat, but in all the time I was out there, I never was afraid, and I was sometimes alone for three and four days at a time while my eldest girl stayed in town and cooked for the boys."

Sophie is still here today, working and struggling with all her might. She and her son William always made certain to rip out any strangler fig seedling before it became too rooted in a cabbage palm around their house. That's how we all survived back then, by ripping out the stranglers from our lives.

The Wueppers and the Zills are still here, and Carrie Frey has been married to William Zill for eighteen years already. Adolf has taken such a liking to their son Laurence because the boy is so interested in plants and trees. Adolf has spent considerable time showing Laurence how to graft mango trees by the in-arching, or in-bottle method, as it is called. They use a turpentine mango tree for rootstock, then take graft wood from a hybrid mango tree, such as a Haden, and graft the two together in a Castoria bottle filled with water. It's a long, slow process, but Adolf likes to help Laurence since the young man has such a keen interest and wants to start his own nursery some day. He wants to develop his own variety of mango that he plans to name the Zill mango.

As I was reminiscing about the old days, I went up to the attic to search for Adolf's old copy of the original map of Linton drawn in 1895. As I looked closely at the map in the dim light coming through the film of cobwebs in the attic window, I saw that the surveyor had even sketched the sour orange trees, gone these many years, just south of Atlantic Avenue near Ocean Boulevard. On the map I discovered a large circle, or roundabout, named Palmetto Park, which he had originally designed to curve north and south of Atlantic Avenue, one block west of Ocean Boulevard. It was never completed.

The map showed that Mr. Flagler and Mr. Linton had also planned a large spur of the Florida East Coast Railway tracks that would sweep on a curve from the main line and head east to the canal. Mr. Thomson had drawn railroad tracks branching off the main line and curving one block north of Atlantic Avenue. Perhaps the three of them had plans for a large resort hotel on the beach with trains that would carry guests to and from the station, or maybe they designed the spur merely to carry crops and haul freight from the canal area. The plans were abandoned, and the railway spur was never built.

This is Adolf's copy of the original town map, surveyed by E. Burslem Thomson in 1895. Thomson sketched in the location of the old sour orange grove south of Atlantic Avenue near the beach. The map also reveals proposed plans and locations in town that were never completed.

On the map my finger traced the length of Atlantic Avenue to the school square. The map called for a large park or public grounds on the entire block south of the school square. Evidently that plan had also been abandoned and forgotten. The rest of the map was precisely drawn. The old town of Linton had grown almost as planned and even expanded beyond the original town limits.

I shut the door to the attic and returned to my needlepoint downstairs. After we finished the church linens several weeks ago, I decided to do some needlepoint for our home. I've been working on a cross-stitch design of the Twenty-third Psalm for some time now, and the lettering and borders are almost finished. First, I stitched a figure of the shepherd standing by the water and the pasture where sheep are grazing. When I was stitching the design of the "still waters" with my blue thread, I couldn't help but think of the small stream that flowed west of the old beach ridge when Delray Beach was known as Zion in 1895. It was a quiet, gentle stream that restored my soul every time I rested there.

It hardly seems possible that the outpost of Zion has vanished, but our old church building, my second Zion, still stands. And the older I get, the more I think of the eternal Zion promised in Scripture. Yet for now, home is here on this same land that's been ours all these years, almost as if we've been grafted to the land and were meant to stay. As Psalm 84 says, we will live out our years "from strength to strength," as best we can, between time and eternity.

My greetings and love to all,
Anna

Later Years

Despite the collapse of an inflated real estate market in 1926 and the devastation of the 1928 Hurricane, Adolf and Anna remained in Delray Beach. They had experienced privation and had inured themselves to the uncertainties of nature and the whims of human nature. The long-anticipated inheritance from the Schwarz estate, eaten up by years of legal fees and maneuvering in the courts, never materialized.

The driving force behind Adolf and Anna was their devotion to the land. Their lives were built upon the solid foundation of faith and family. They continued to live quiet and productive lives as firmly rooted as their mango trees, which defied the decades. As part of the land, they endured.

Of the three children, Annie never married and remained in Delray Beach, taking care of her parents in their home. Well into the 1950s, Aunt Annie continued Grandma's welcome ritual at the front door. Aunt Annie would swish off each caller with her homemade palmetto broom in the age-old battle against the relentless mosquitoes. After her parents' deaths, Annie wisely invested their estate in stocks with advice from C.Y. Byrd and periodically sold off individual lots for additional income. Annie remained in the old house until 1965, when she finally sold it and moved into an apartment owned by Delray Beach pioneer Leona Blank Davis. Under new ownership, the old house burned to the ground that year. Nothing could be salvaged.

Clara went through the eighth grade, which was customary for girls in that day, in the old Delray School. She realized her dream by moving to Miami in 1918 at the age of sixteen. She attended a business school in

Miami and secured a job as a bookkeeper for the Miami Grocery Company. Her mandatory piano lessons proved worthwhile when she later served as pianist for St. Matthew's Lutheran Church in Miami. Later, she married, became a homemaker and the mother of one son, and went on to purchase real estate for rental purposes from time to time.

William also realized his dream and went into banking while attending Twentieth Century Business College in West Palm Beach. He worked as a bookkeeper and assistant cashier at the Bank of Delray for a period of five years. In the late 1920s, he drove his old Model T Ford to New York City with "Ferd" Hartmann, also of Delray Beach. There, William worked as a teller at the Seaboard National Bank, which later merged with Chase Manhattan Bank. Returning to Florida in 1929, he worked as a teller at the First National Bank of Miami run by the demanding Edward and Mildred Romfh, two of Miami's most colorful characters. In 1931 Mr. Romfh promoted William and sent him to join the newly formed First National Bank of Hollywood, Florida, where he rose to become president of the bank and vice-chairman of the Board of Directors. William and his wife had three children.

Requiem

Over the decades Adolf and Anna continued to live in their house built in 1896. As Delray Beach grew, they watched the town they once knew gradually change and disappear. The quiet canal was widened and became the Intracoastal Waterway. Tomato fields were replaced by automobile dealerships, and pineapple patches were plowed under to make way for downtown buildings. The

secluded, meandering Hofman Lane was renamed Palm Trail, and Hofman Avenue became Northeast Seventh Street. Their lifetime ebbed slowly in ordained, disciplined order. The years drifted by like orange blossoms blown by the wind.

On July 7, 1945, Anna passed away quietly at the age of seventy-one. At her funeral in the small church she saw built and damaged by the 1928 Hurricane, she lay in repose beneath the glowing stained glass window of the Good Shepherd, which she and Adolf had donated. Robed in the radiant splendor of stained glass, the Good Shepherd stood watching over her and led her into green pastures beside the still waters. In life she had moved from strength to strength in the outpost once named Zion; in death she found her final Zion.

In his later years, Adolf became totally blind as a result of hemorrhaging in both eyes after cataract surgery. Annie became his caregiver and constant companion, driving him back and forth to church and keeping him aware of the latest happenings in Delray Beach. As the years progressed, he remained alert and keenly interested in the development of Delray Beach. On October 18, 1953, fifty-eight years after his arrival at the Orange Grove House of Refuge, Adolf passed away at the age of eighty-two.

Over the years, Annie, Clara, and William gradually sold parts of Adolf's original property a little at a time with the same cautious concern for the land evidenced by Adolf and Anna. Annie died on February 7, 1982. In her will she left a bequest to Trinity Evangelical Lutheran Church that helped build the Hofman Center for Christian Education, a two-story wing of Trinity Lutheran School on North Swinton Avenue.

For decades Adolf and Anna's land proved productive in yielding vegetables, pineapples, bananas, and mangoes. It withstood frost, hurricanes, unscrupulous real estate developers, and the crash of property values in 1926. The land outlasted Linton and silently witnessed the birth and development of Delray Beach over a period of ten decades.

Epilogue

Of the original sixty acres purchased by Adolf in 1895, only one lot remained in the Hofman family in 1995. Abandoned and alone, the old pump Adolf brought to Linton stood engulfed in a grove of decaying mango trees whose broad canopy covered the last vanishing traces of the Hofman homestead. The old circular driveway had disappeared beneath layers and layers of dried leaves. Eight gnarled and burled mango trees, the last of Adolf's groves, stood as silent sentinels towering over the ruins of his packing house. Broken and bowed by the years, they still bore fruit in their season and thrust their new wine-colored leaves to the sky as if greeting Adolf and Anna anew each year, heralding their long-fulfilled dreams. When this last piece of the Hofman homestead was sold and the trees torn down, the last of the land that was Linton vanished into history.

Bibliography

Britt, Lora Sinks. "Builders of Delray." *Delray Beach Journal*. 2nd in a series, Feb. 3, 1949.

_____. *My Gold Coast*. Palatka, Florida: Brittany House Publishers, 1984.

Burnett, Gene M. *Florida's Past*. Sarasota: Pineapple Press, Inc., 1998.

Diggans, Leroy. *History of Delray*. Delray. Florida: unpublished.

Farrar, Cecil W. and Margoann. *Incomparable Delray Beach - Early Life and Lore*. Boynton Beach, Florida: Starr Publishing Company, Inc., 1971.

Florida East Coast: General Information. (General Information Booklet Published by the Florida East Coast Railway). St. Augustine: The Record Company, 1906.

Frey, Carrie. *Diary, 1908-1910*. Delray: Unpublished original manuscript, 1910.

Frey, Sophie. *Life's Bitter Sweet - An Autobiography*. Delray: Unpublished original manuscript, 1930.

Keen, R.C. "Seven Men Founded Delray Beach in 1895." *Delray Beach News*. Oct. 4, 1940, Vol. XVIII, No. 9, p. 1.

Kingsbury, Frank Burnside. compiler, *The City of Delray, Florida: (Notes on the History of the City of Delray, Florida, Comprising Notes Compiled From Original Sources.)* Keene, New Hampshire: Unpublished, 1935.

Kuolt, Milton C. *Seventy-five Years of Memories: A History of Trinity Evangelical Lutheran Church*. Hackensack, New Jersey: Custombook, Inc., 1979.

Lauther, Olive Chapman. *The Lonesome Road*. Miami: Center Printing Co., 1963.

McGoun, William E. *Southeast Florida Pioneers: The Palm and Treasure Coasts*. Sarasota: Pineapple Press, Inc., 1998.

McIver, Stuart B. *Yesterday's Palm Beach Including Palm Beach County*. Miami: E.A. Seemann Publishing, Inc., 1976.

Norris, Jan. "The Zill Family Tree." *Palm Beach Post*. July 11, 1996, Sect. FN, p. 1.

Peebles. "Interview with Adolf Hofman." January 22, 1937.

Peters, Thelma. *Biscayne Country: 1870-1926*. Miami: Banyan Books, Inc., 1981.

Pierce, Charles W. *Pioneer Life in South Florida*. Ed. Donald Walter Curl. Coral Gables: University of Miami Press, 1970.

Reeves, Linda. *Delray's Ghost Ship*. Delray Beach: Sea Scripts, Inc., 1993.

Tropical Sun, West Palm Beach, Florida. March 20, 1913, p. 2.